Sedona's G

MW00929475

AN EASY-TO-USE GUIDE
FOR 55+ HIKING TRAILS and LOOP
HIKES IN SEDONA, ARIZONA

FEATURING
20 FAVORITE HIKING TRAILS
and LOOP HIKES

by
William Bohan

Non-liability Statement

The author has taken every precaution to ensure that the information contained within is up-to-date, accurate and reflects trail conditions when this guide was printed. However, trail conditions frequently change because of weather, Forest Service activity or other causes. The included GPS data were obtained from a Garmin model 60CSx GPS unit. Because the location, elevation and track data are only as accurate as the sensitivity of the GPS unit, some inaccuracies may be present. Everyone, including users of GPS data, is urged to use common sense when hiking. Always stay on the trail. The author, publisher, contributors, and all those involved in the preparation of this guide, either directly or indirectly, disclaim any liability for injuries, accidents, and damages whatsoever that may occur to those using this guide. You are responsible for your health and safety while hiking the trails.

Acknowledgments

The author would like to acknowledge several individuals for their contributions to this guide. They are:

Lorna Thompson and Nancy Williams for editing this work; Brenda Andrusyszyn, Michelle Barrett, Carole Bell, Wade Bell, David Butler, Ruth Butler, Barbara Lewis, Peg Likens, Tom Likens, Barbara Livermont, Gary Livermont, Cindy Parker, Rene' Ragan, Rick Ragan, Jim Rostedt, Kathy Rostedt, Gary Stouder, Barrie Thomas, Grace Thomas, Darryl Thompson, Lorna Thompson and Marjorie Whitton for their companionship while hiking the trails.

© **Copyright William Bohan 2020 - 2023**

All rights reserved
No portion of this guide may be reproduced in whole or in part by any means (with the exception of short quotes for the purpose of review), without the express permission of the author. v 1.15

Cover Photo enjoying the view from the top of Doe Mountain

Table of Contents

Features of This Guide

Sedona's Greatest Hikes contains all the information you need to have a wonderful hiking experience in Sedona, Arizona. It includes the best, but not all trails in the Sedona area. Driving distances shown on the maps are from the "Y." The trail descriptions give you the highlights of each trail, what to watch for and where to take the best photos. A representative photo of each trail and easy-to-understand maps are included.

QR Code Technology

Because of space limitations, only one representative color photograph from each trail is included in this guide. But by using QR code technology, you can scan the QR code found near each trail map which will give you access to additional color photos of each trail.

Definition of Cumulative Ascent

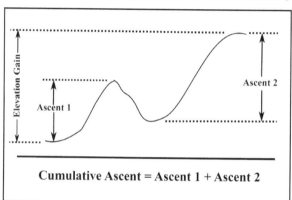

Cumulative Ascent = Ascent 1 + Ascent 2

Sedona hiking trails are not flat, but rather rise and fall over their length. You'll find cumulative ascent rather than elevation change on each trail/loop map. Cumulative ascent reflects the total of all the ups of the trail. The greater the cumulative ascent, the more difficult the trail becomes. Elevation change reflects the difference between the lowest and highest elevations of the trail. Cumulative ascent is always greater than the elevation change.

Hiking Time

Hiking time is estimated based on a hiking speed of between 1.5 and 2 miles per hour. Trails that have greater cumulative ascent are at the lower end of that range to allow for stops to catch your breath. Hiking time doesn't include stops for snacks, photographs, meditation, etc.

Trail Popularity

A popular trail is indicated by 4 🚶🚶🚶🚶 symbols. You'll find just one 🚶 symbol for a trail that isn't used very often. You should expect crowds on trails with 4 hiker symbols and likely won't encounter other hikers on a trail that has just one hiker symbol. Weekends in Sedona bring more hikers to the trails and holidays can be especially busy.

In-Out Hikes vs. Loop Hikes

For an in-out hike (e.g. Fay Canyon), you'll hike a trail for a distance then retrace your steps to return to the trailhead. A loop hike is a circular hike using either a single trail (e.g. Baldwin Loop) or a combination of several trails and you essentially won't retrace your steps as you return to the trailhead.

Trailhead Shuttle Service

A free trailhead shuttle service has been launched to help alleviate trailhead parking lot overcrowding at the Soldier Pass, Dry Creek, Mescal, Cathedral Rock and Little Horse trailheads. The shuttles operate Thursday, Friday, Saturday and Sunday from 8:00 am to 6:30 pm and on additional days during busy times. The shuttles are free and a Red Rock Pass is not required to hike. Restrooms are available at each shuttle park and ride lot. Parking is prohibited at the Cathedral Rock and Soldier Pass trailheads when the shuttles are running. There are three trailhead park and ride shuttle parking lots.

The **West SR89A Park & Ride** lot located at 905 Upper Red Rock Loop Road has shuttles serving the **Mescal** (number **3** on the map below) and **Dry Creek** (number **2** on the map below) trailheads

The **Posse Grounds Park & Ride** lot located at 20 Carruth Drive, off of Soldiers Pass Road has shuttles serving the **Soldier Pass (1)** and **Dry Creek (2)** trailheads. This Park & Ride lot can also be used to access the shared use path alongside Soldiers Pass Road so that you can hike about 1 mile to the **Soldier Pass** trailhead (see Soldier Pass Trail).

The **North SR 179 Park & Ride** lot located at 1294 SR 179, off of Bowstring Drive has shuttles serving the **Cathedral Rock (4)** and **Little Horse (5)** trailheads.

Complete information about the trailhead shuttles, including real-time departure information is available at www.SedonaShuttle.com. You can also download the Transloc App from Google Play and the App Store for real-time departure information.

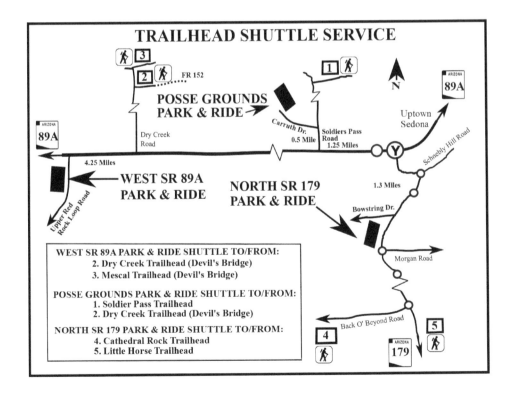

Vortex Information

If you come to Sedona with the thought of visiting a vortex or two, you are not alone. It's estimated that more than half of Sedona visitors are interested in experiencing the power of vortexes (vortices). There are four well known Sedona vortexes: Airport, Bell Rock, Boynton Canyon, and Cathedral Rock. All four locations are described in this guidebook. There are other areas, several of which are shown below, that are considered by some to be powerful vortex areas. I suggest that you approach each vortex without preconceived ideas of what you may experience and just let the experience happen. If nothing else, you'll enjoy some of Sedona's finest views.

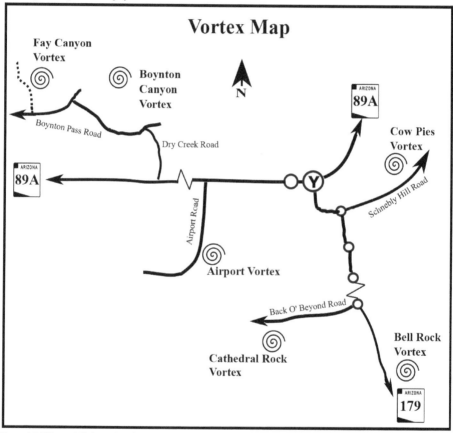

If you'd like additional information on the four well known vortexes, plus information on the location of 10 lesser known power spots where vortex energy has been reported, you might be interested in *Hiking the Vortexes, a* book that is available at many Sedona retailers or scan the code below.

Safe Hiking Tips

The stunning, unique red rock formations, moderate temperatures, low humidity and close proximity to the trails make hiking in Sedona an experience unlike anywhere else in the world. But hiking is not without risk. It is very important to be prepared, even for a day hike. Bring enough water to stay hydrated and drink water throughout the hike. In addition:

- Check the weather before you begin hiking and reschedule your hike if inclement weather is predicted
- Wear a hat and sunscreen and take along a wind breaker or light raincoat
- Bring hiking poles as they may help with balance on the uneven trails
- Wear hiking boots or sturdy walking shoes with good grip as the trails can be uneven, rocky and slippery
- Carry a first-aid kit, a fully charged cell phone (although many hiking trails do not have cell phone service), flashlight, compass, hiking guide, map, portable GPS unit, rescue whistle, pocketknife and a snack
- Hike with at least one other person and complete the hike before sunset
- If you must hike alone, let someone know where you'll be hiking and leave a note in your vehicle stating where you intend to hike and when you expect to return
- Trailhead parking areas can be the target of thieves so don't leave valuables in your vehicle
- Stay on the designated trail. Most rescues are for hikers who have left the trail to "explore"
- Downhill hikers have the right-of-way in most instances because footing is more tenuous downhill than uphill. If hiking uphill, step aside and let downhill hikers pass
- Mountain bikers are supposed to yield to all trail users, but use common sense and step aside when appropriate
- There is no trash service in the forest. Take out anything you bring in. "Take nothing but pictures, leave nothing but footprints"

Definition of the "Y"

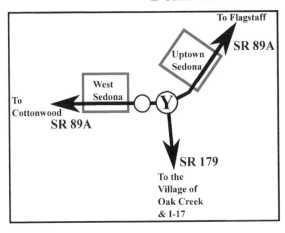

If you obtain directions from a Sedona local, chances they will give you those directions referencing something called the "Y." The "Y" is also used as the reference point in this guidebook. The "Y" is the traffic circle at the intersection of State Route (SR) 89A and SR 179, which is west of Uptown Sedona and east of West Sedona. All of the driving distances shown on the maps are from the "Y."

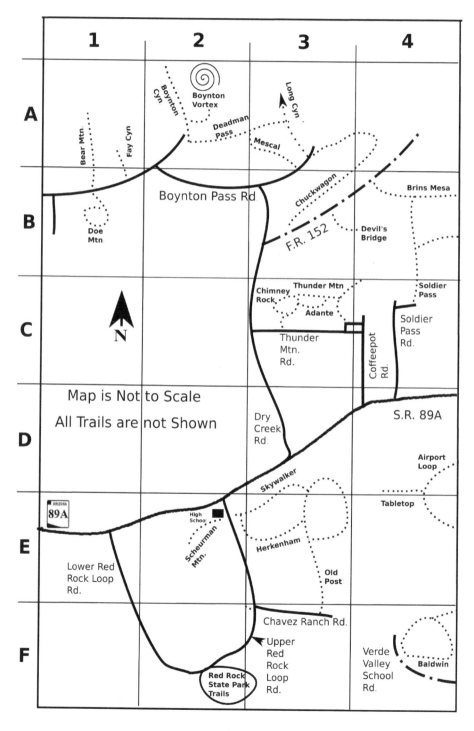

Loops Closest to Sedona

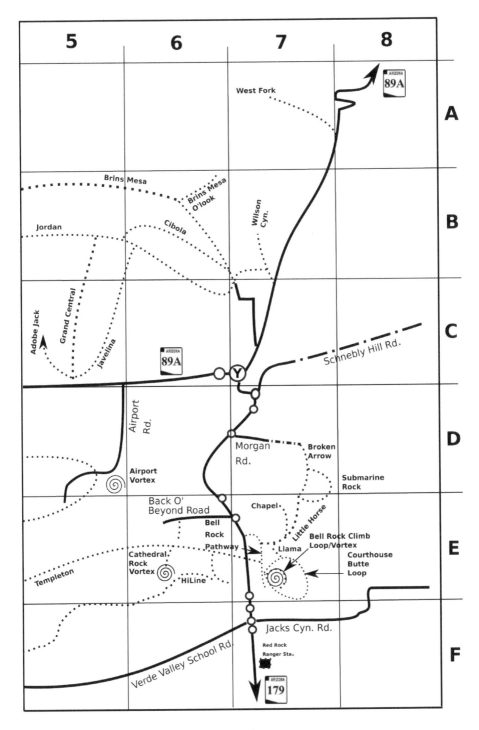

Sedona Average Weather & Sunrise/Sunset Data

	Temperature (°F)		Precipitation	Sunrise	Sunset
	High	Low	(Inches)	(1st of	Month)
January	55	30	1.7	7:35 AM	5:39 PM
February	59	32	1.5	7:13 AM	6:10 PM
March	63	35	1.7	6:37 AM	6:36 PM
April	72	42	1.2	5:55 AM	7:00 PM
May	81	49	0.6	5:23 AM	7:24 PM
June	91	57	0.5	5:13 AM	7:43 PM
July	95	65	1.9	5:25 AM	7:41 PM
August	92	64	2.4	5:48 AM	7:15 PM
September	88	58	1.5	6:10 AM	6:33 PM
October	78	48	1.1	6:33 AM	5:52 PM
November	65	37	1.3	7:02 AM	5:22 PM
December	56	30	1.7	7:27 AM	5:18 PM
Average	75	46	1.4		

GPS Data

When you read the trail descriptions, you will find numbers in brackets such as {1}, {2} etc. These numbers refer to points of interest shown on the maps and mentioned in the trail descriptions.

GPS data in the universal gpx format for the trails contained in this guidebook are available at: https://greatsedonahikes.com/gps/gps.html or scan the code below.

Photographic Hotspots

You'll find camera symbols 📷 on many of the maps. While photographic opportunities are remarkable on all the trails, the camera symbol indicates some of the best locations to take photos of the red rocks or other interesting scenery.

Red Rock Pass Fee Program

If you park on the National Forest around Sedona, you may need to display a Recreation Pass. If you stop temporarily on the National Forest to take a photo remaining near your vehicle, you probably don't need to display a Recreation Pass.

A Recreation Pass is required for trailhead parking for many of the trails listed in this guide. It is also required for the Bootlegger, Banjo Bill, Halfway and Encinoso picnic areas in Oak Creek Canyon. Additionally, there are 3 special fee areas: Crescent Moon Ranch/Red Rock Crossing, West Fork Trail (Call O' the Canyon), and Grasshopper Point Picnic Area. Each area charges a separate, unique fee. Developed campgrounds have their own fees.

A Recreation Pass is: 1) A National Parks Pass, also known as a Federal Interagency Annual Pass 2) A Senior Pass, also known as a Federal Interagency Senior Pass available to U.S. residents 62 years of age and older 3) A Federal Interagency Access Pass issued to individuals with permanent disabilities 4) A Red Rock Pass (described below).

If you do not have any of the above Federal Interagency Passes, you may display a **Red Rock Pass**, available for sale at many Sedona-area businesses, the Red Rock Ranger Station Visitor Center, the Sedona Chamber of Commerce Uptown Visitor Center and selected trailheads. The Red Rock Pass is available as a $5 Daily Pass, a $15 Weekly Pass, a $20 Annual Pass, or a $40 Grand Annual Pass. The machines located at the trailheads accept credit cards or cash ($1, $5 and $10) and only issue Daily or Weekly Red Rock Passes.

- The $5 Daily Red Rock Pass permits you to park on the National Forest for one calendar day. It expires at midnight. It does not include the additional parking fees at the 3 special fee areas.
- The $15 Weekly Red Rock Pass permits you to park on the National Forest for 7 consecutive days. It does not include the additional parking fees at the 3 special fee areas.
- The $20 Annual Red Rock Pass permits you to park on the National Forest for 12 consecutive months. It does not include the additional parking fees at the 3 special fee areas.
- The $40 Grand Annual Pass permits you to park on the National Forest and includes the additional parking fees at the 3 special fee areas for 12 consecutive months. It is available at the Red Rock Ranger Station and the Sedona Chamber of Commerce Uptown Visitor Center.

The Red Rock Pass Program changes periodically For the latest information, check http://www.fs.usda.gov/main/coconino/passes-permits/recreation or scan the code below.

To hike the trails at the Red Rock State Park, you'll pay a separate additional admission fee at the entrance station.

Alphabetical List of Included Hiking Trails/Loop Hikes

★ symbol = Favorite Trail/Loop
(RRSP) = Trail at the Red Rock State Park

Alphabetical List of Included Hiking Trails/Loop Hikes (Cont'd)

List of 20 Favorite Hiking Trails/Loop Hikes

★ symbol = Favorite Trail/Loop
(RRSP) = Trail at the Red Rock State Park

Alphabetical List of Included Loop Hikes

Hiking Trails/Loop Hikes Listed By Difficulty

Easy

Easy to Moderate

Moderate

★ symbol = Favorite Trail/Loop

Hiking Trails/Loop Hikes Listed By Difficulty (Cont'd)

Hiking Trails/Loop Hikes Listed By Feature

Shaded Hiking Trails/Loop Hikes for Hot Weather

The following trails provide partial shade and may be suitable for summer hiking. But be sure to take extra water when hiking in the summer.

Hiking Trails/Loop Hikes for Muddy Conditions

After rain or snow, the following trails may be suitable for hiking. Do not hike if thunderstorm, lightning or flash flood warnings are present.

Airport Loop and Airport Vortex

Summary: A loop hike that circles the Sedona Airport with nice views all around and a chance to visit one of Sedona's famous vortexes

Challenge Level: Easy for the vortex hike; Moderate for the loop hike

Hiking Distance: From the Airport Road parking area {1} less than 0.25 mile round trip for the vortex; about 3.3 miles for the loop hike, add another 1 mile if you hike the Tabletop Trail. Add 1.2 miles to all the above mileages if you hike from the Sedona View parking area {2}.

Hiking Time: From the Airport Road parking area, about ½ hour round trip for the vortex; about 2 hours for the Airport Loop hike: add ½ hour for the Tabletop Trail. From the Sedona View parking area, add 1 hour to the above estimated hiking times.

Trail Popularity: For the vortex: 🚶🚶 🚶🚶 🚶🚶 🚶🚶 For the loop hike: 🚶🚶 🚶🚶

Trailhead Directions: There are two ways to access this trail. From the "Y" roundabout (see page 7), drive west toward Cottonwood on SR 89A for 1 mile then turn left onto Airport Road, which is the first traffic light west of the "Y." The primary trailhead is located approximately 0.5 mile up Airport Road on the left {1}. (34°51.345'N; 111°46.804'W) There is parking for 10 vehicles plus one handicapped spot here.

If the parking lot is full, continue on for 0.6 mile then turn left into the Scenic Overlook parking area. The Sedona View trailhead is at the northeast corner of the parking area {2}. (34°51.196'N; 111°47.372'W) There is a $3 parking fee at this parking area.

Description: If you park on Airport Road {1}, you can easily reach one of Sedona's famous vortexes. From the parking area continue past the first sign then follow the main trail east until you come to a second sign in about 200 feet {3}. Turn left here then follow the trail to Overlook Point for a short distance then make a right turn to climb up about 50 feet to the overlook. The top of the rock formation is Overlook Point and is considered to be the vortex {4}. (Additional information on vortexes can be found on page 6.) From the Scenic View parking area {2}, hike the Sedona View Trail downhill for 0.6 mile. Continue past the intersection with the Airport Loop Trail to the intersection with the sign for Overlook Point {3} to go to the vortex {4}.

As you hike the Airport Loop Trail, there are good views all around. On the east, there are great views of Twin Buttes and, to the south, Cathedral Rock. Be sure to hike the 0.5 mile Tabletop Trail at the southwest end of the runway {5} to the end of the mesa {6} for a spectacular view of Sedona's Pyramid. Return to the Airport Loop Trail where after 0.6 mile you'll intersect the Bandit Trail {7} and have nice views of Chimney Rock, Thunder Mountain and Coffeepot Rock on the north side of the loop. You'll cross Airport Road to return to the parking area

Note: This trail is very rocky and has narrow sections with large drop offs.

Color Photos: Scan the QR code below for additional color photos of this trail

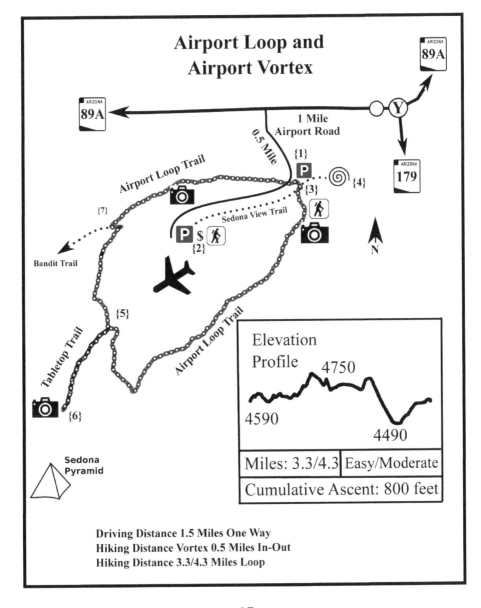

Airport Loop and Airport Vortex

ARIZONA **89A**

ARIZONA **89A**

1 Mile
Airport Road

0.5 Mile

{1}

Airport Loop Trail

{7}

Sedona View Trail

{3}

{4}

ARIZONA **179**

N

{2}

Bandit Trail

Tabletop Trail

{5}

Airport Loop Trail

{6}

Sedona
Pyramid

Elevation Profile 4750

4590

4490

Miles: 3.3/4.3	Easy/Moderate
Cumulative Ascent: 800 feet	

Driving Distance 1.5 Miles One Way
Hiking Distance Vortex 0.5 Miles In-Out
Hiking Distance 3.3/4.3 Miles Loop

Baldwin Loop ★

Summary: A favorite loop trail at the base of Cathedral Rock offering some excellent views with an optional short side trip to the banks of Oak Creek

Challenge Level: Moderate

Hiking Distance: About a 2.7 mile loop

Hiking Time: About 1½ hours round trip

Trail Popularity: 🚶🚶🚶

Trailhead Directions: The trailhead is located on the unpaved portion of Verde Valley School Road. From the "Y" roundabout (see page 7), drive south on SR 179 about 7 miles to the Jacks Canyon/Verde Valley School Road roundabout then take the first exit onto Verde Valley School Road. At 4 miles, you'll pass the Turkey Creek parking area on your left {10} and at 4.5 miles you'll see the Baldwin Trail parking area on the left (west) side of Verde Valley School Road {1}. (34°49.309'N; 111°48.493'W) The trailhead is across the road from the north end of the parking area. There are toilets at the parking area.

Description: Named for Andrew Baldwin, one of the individuals who bought Crescent Moon Ranch in 1936, the Baldwin Loop Trail circles an unnamed red rock butte and provides excellent views of Cathedral Rock. After crossing the road, you'll come to a signboard {2}. You can hike the Baldwin Trail in either clockwise or counter clockwise direction. If you hike in the clockwise direction, you'll intersect a social trail in 0.3 mile {3} and the Templeton Trail after 0.5 mile {4}. Take a side trip by hiking east on the Templeton Trail until it is beside Oak Creek. After 0.2 mile, look across Oak Creek to see Buddha Beach, where visitors use river rock to build amazing stacked structures {5}. Periodically, floods knock the structures down, but they are usually quickly rebuilt. You may be lucky and see hundreds of buddhas. If you continue east on the Templeton Trail for 0.8 mile, you'll intersect the Cathedral Rock Trail.

Return to the Baldwin Loop Trail intersection then turn left to continue around the tall red rock butte. You'll pass some excellent places to stop and enjoy the views {6} {8} on your loop. You'll intersect the HiLine Trail {7}, which is a popular mountain biking trail, and a spur off of the Baldwin Loop Trail {9} that leads across Verde Valley School Road to the Turkey Creek Trail parking area {10}. For the best photos of Cathedral Rock, do this hike later in the day.

Color Photos: Scan the QR code below for additional color photos of this trail

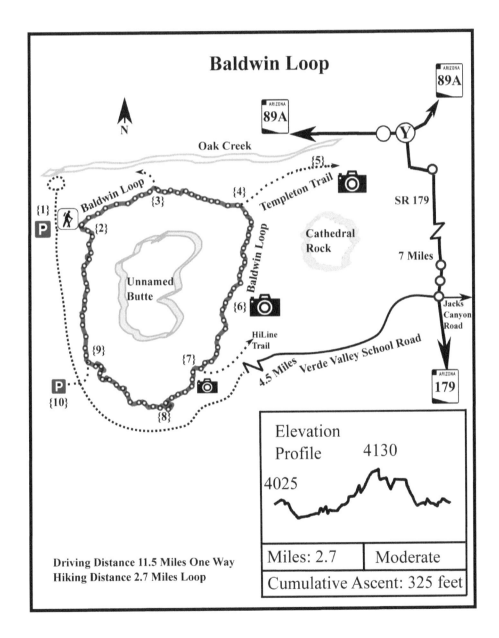

Bear Mountain Trail ★

Summary: A favorite strenuous, sunny, in-out hike with excellent red rock views

Challenge Level: Hard

Hiking Distance: About 2.4 miles each way to the top of Bear Mountain or 4.8 miles round trip

Hiking Time: About 4 hours round trip

Trail Popularity: 🚶🚶

Trailhead Directions: From the "Y" roundabout (see page 7), drive west toward Cottonwood on SR 89A about 3 miles. Turn right onto Dry Creek Road. Stay on Dry Creek Road to a stop sign (about 3 miles) then turn left onto Boynton Pass Road. Proceed about 1.6 miles to a stop sign. Turn left and continue on Boynton Pass Road. The trailhead parking {1} is the second parking area on the left side, about 1.8 miles from the stop sign. (34°53.596'N; 111°51.945'W) This parking area also serves the Doe Mountain Trail. The Bear Mountain Trail begins across the road from the parking area. There are toilets at the parking area.

Description: Bear Mountain provides fantastic views of near and far red rock formations. You'll be hiking a trail with a cumulative ascent of some 2100 feet. This makes Bear Mountain a hard hike.

After crossing the road and stepping over a low fence, you first cross a series of three deep washes and enter a meadow-like landscape. After 0.3 mile, you begin the climb up the mountain. Throughout the hike, be sure to look around to enjoy the great views. After 0.7 mile you'll come to a huge rock beside the trail {2}.

At 1.2 miles, you'll come to a flat area {3} and soon have to scramble up in a narrow slot. At 1.4 miles, you'll reach a summit {4} then begin a series of descents and ascents. At 2 miles, you'll come to a large area of slick rock {5}, soon followed by a natural stopping place and photo opportunity at elevation 6150 feet {6}.

To reach the very top of Bear Mountain, you'll hike an additional 0.4 mile with ascents and descents. From the top of Bear Mountain {7}, look north and you can see the San Francisco Peaks northwest of Flagstaff.

Note: The trail is fairly easy to follow and there are usually cairns placed by other hikers. The trail is rocky with exposed and extreme drop-offs in some parts – watch your footing. Take extra water in the summer as there is limited shade and it can be a hot hike.

Color Photos: Scan the QR code below for additional color photos of this trail

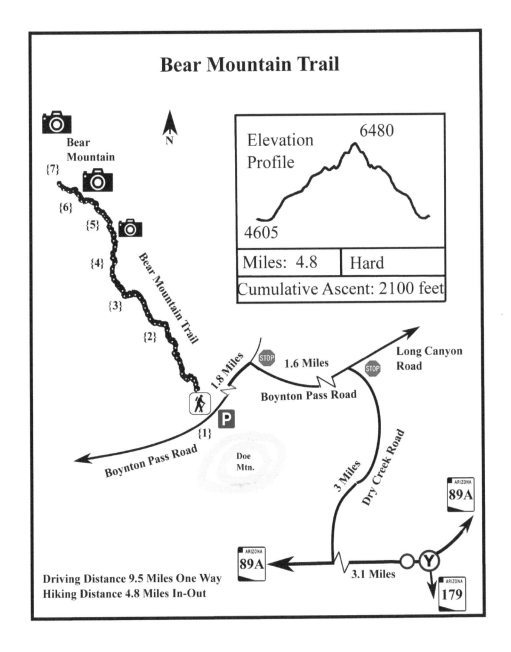

Bell Rock Climb and Bell Rock Vortex

Summary: Explore a famous Sedona rock formation and perhaps experience some vortex energy

Challenge Level: Easy but watch your footing

Hiking Distance: About 1.2 miles round trip

Hiking Time: About 1 hour round trip

Trail Popularity: 🏃🏃 🏃🏃 🏃🏃 🏃🏃

Trailhead Directions: From the "Y" roundabout (see page 7), drive south on SR 179 for about 5 miles to the parking area. After you drive about 3.2 miles, just past the Back O' Beyond roundabout, SR 179 becomes a divided highway. Continue driving south. About 1.8 miles beyond the Back O' Beyond roundabout, southbound SR 179 adds a passing lane on the left. From the passing lane, turn left at the sign for the Court House Vista parking area {1}. (34°48.350'N; 111°46.009'W) Before you turn, you'll see Bell Rock ahead of you on the left side of SR 179. This parking area also serves the Bell Rock Loop, Courthouse Butte Loop, Templeton and Llama Trails. There are toilets at the parking area. The trail starts just beyond the interpretive signboard.

Description: After you park in the Court House Vista parking area, walk past the interpretive signboard then proceed straight ahead on the Bell Rock Trail. Follow it for 0.2 mile to the intersection with the Bell Rock Pathway (BRP) Trail {2}. Continue straight ahead then make a slight left onto the Bell Rock Climb. In about 0.1 mile (and after climbing up about 65 feet), you'll intersect the Rector Connector Trail {3}. Make a right turn then continue to follow Bell Rock Climb and you'll shortly come to a large relatively flat area {4}.

You'll note that Bell Rock Climb goes to the left and right. If you go left, you'll go the east side of Bell Rock and have excellent views of Lee Mountain and Courthouse Butte. The trail becomes very narrow with large drop offs so I recommend you turn around after about 0.1 mile {5}. But take a few minutes to enjoy the views. Then return to where you came up on Bell Rock Climb and proceed to the west on the large flat area. Vortex energy has been reported all over Bell Rock so you may feel the energy. (Additional information on vortexes can be found on page 6.)

After about 0.8 mile, you'll come to a cairn and see that just beyond the cairn, there is a trail on the slick rock continuing around Bell Rock {6}. If you want to climb up to a vortex area known as the Meditation Perch, follow the slick rock around Bell Rock and you'll see the Meditation Perch ahead {7}. After you visit Meditation Perch, return to the cairn {6} then make a left turn to descend Bell Rock. You'll see Bell Rock Pathway below so make a right turn {8} then follow Bell Rock Pathway for 0.1 mile then make a left turn onto to the Bell Rock Trail {2} to return to the parking area {1}.

Note: You'll see several cairns above you high up on Bell Rock. A scramble up to these cairns requires steep climbs on smooth rocks. If you attempt, be extremely careful.

Color Photos: Scan the QR code below for additional color photos of this trail

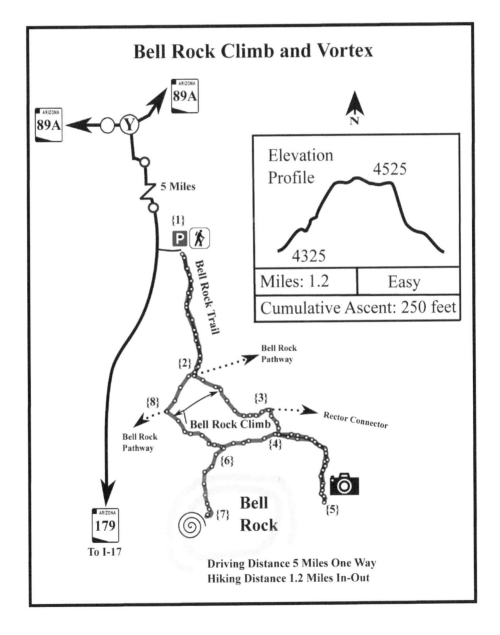

Bell Rock Climb and Vortex

Elevation Profile

4525

4325

Miles: 1.2	Easy
Cumulative Ascent: 250 feet	

89A

89A

5 Miles

{1}

Bell Rock Trail

Bell Rock Pathway

{2}

{8}

{3}

Rector Connector

Bell Rock Climb

Bell Rock Pathway

{4}

{6}

179

To I-17

{7}

Bell Rock

{5}

Driving Distance 5 Miles One Way
Hiking Distance 1.2 Miles In-Out

Bell Rock Loop ★

Summary: A favorite easy loop hike that circles Bell Rock

Challenge Level: Easy

Hiking Distance: About 1.9 miles loop

Hiking Time: About 1 hour round trip

Trail Popularity:

Trailhead Directions: From the "Y" roundabout (see page 7), drive south on SR 179 for about 5 miles to the parking area. After you drive about 3.2 miles, just past the Back O' Beyond roundabout, SR 179 becomes a divided highway. Continue driving south. About 1.8 miles beyond the Back O' Beyond roundabout, southbound SR 179 adds a passing lane on the left. From the passing lane, turn left at the sign for the Court House Vista parking area {1}. (34°48.350'N; 111°46.009'W) Before you turn, you'll see Bell Rock ahead of you on the left side of SR 179. This parking area also serves the Bell Rock Climb, Courthouse Butte Loop, Templeton and Llama Trails. There are toilets at the parking area. The trail starts just beyond the interpretive signboard.

Description: After you park in the Court House Vista parking area, walk past the interpretive signboard then proceed straight ahead on the Bell Rock Trail. Follow it for 0.2 mile to the intersection with the Bell Rock Pathway (BRP) Trail {2}. Continue straight ahead and make a slight left onto the Bell Rock Climb to hike the loop in a clockwise direction. In about 0.1 mile (and after climbing up about 65 feet), you'll intersect the Rector Connector Trail {3}. Make a left turn here then continue on the Rector Connector Trail. You'll come to a nice view area in about another 0.1 mile {4} then the trail makes a left turn {5}. The views from the Rector Connector Trail are very nice throughout its length. At 1 mile, you'll intersect the Courthouse Butte Loop Trail {6}. Make a right turn onto Courthouse Butte Loop then follow it for another 0.2 mile then make another right turn onto Bell Rock Pathway {7}.

Proceed on the Bell Rock Pathway for another 0.6 mile and you'll come to the western end of the Bell Rock Climb {8}. Continue on for another 0.1 mile then turn left onto the Bell Rock Trail {2} back to the parking lot {1}. If you don't mind a steep descent, hike the loop in the counterclockwise direction.

Color Photos: Scan the QR code below for additional color photos of this trail

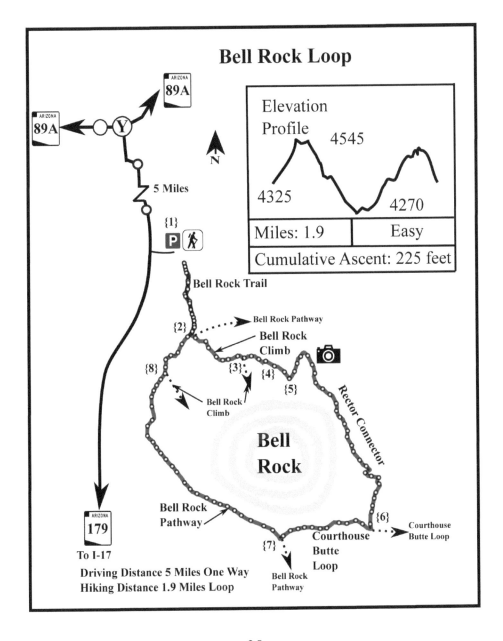

Bell Rock Loop

Elevation Profile	
Miles: 1.9	Easy
Cumulative Ascent: 225 feet	

4545
4325
4270

Bell Rock Trail
Bell Rock Pathway
Bell Rock Climb
{1} P
{2}
{8} {3} {4} {5}
Bell Rock Climb
Rector Connector

Bell Rock

{6}
Courthouse Butte Loop
Bell Rock Pathway
Courthouse Butte Loop
{7}
Bell Rock Pathway

ARIZONA 89A
ARIZONA 89A
Y
5 Miles
N

ARIZONA 179
To I-17

Driving Distance 5 Miles One Way
Hiking Distance 1.9 Miles Loop

Bell Rock Pathway/Templeton Loop

Summary: A loop hike with views of many of Sedona's rock formations

Challenge Level: Moderate

Hiking Distance: About 4.1 miles loop

Hiking Time: About 2 1/2 hours round trip

Trail Popularity:

Trailhead Directions: From the "Y" roundabout (see page 7), drive south on SR 179 about 3.5 miles. Just past the Back O' Beyond roundabout, you'll see a Scenic View sign and a hiking sign on the right side of SR 179 and a left turn lane on the left. Turn left here then proceed to the parking area {1}. (34°49.433'N; 111°46.555'W) The parking area also serves the HT/Easy Breezy Loop and Little Horse Trail. There are toilets at the parking area. Parking is limited at these popular trails. Rather than attempting to park at the trailhead, a better choice is to take the shuttle **(see Trailhead Shuttle Service page 5)** if the parking area is full.

Description: Go past the interpretive signboard then proceed south on the Bell Rock Pathway. You'll intersect the Little Horse trail after 0.3 mile on the left {2}. In another 0.2 mile, you'll cross a footbridge and see the HT Trail sign on the right {3}. You'll be returning on the HT Trail. As you continue on the Bell Rock Pathway, you are rewarded with excellent views of Lee Mountain, Bell Rock and Courthouse Butte.

You'll intersect the Bail Trail {4} after 1.2 miles on the left. After 1.75 miles, you'll intersect the Templeton Trail on the right {5}. Turn right here onto the Templeton Trail. Follow the Templeton Trail beneath both the northbound and southbound lanes of SR 179 then you'll intersect the Easy Breezy Trail for the first time {6}. Continue on the Templeton Trail.

Look around for excellent views of Bell Rock, Courthouse Butte, Lee Mountain, Cathedral Rock and many other red rock formations. At 2.4 miles, you'll intersect the Easy Breezy Trail a second time {7}. At 2.75 miles, you'll have the best view of Cathedral Rock {8}. At 3 miles, you'll intersect the HT Trail on your right {9}. Turn right here then follow the HT Trail. You'll intersect the Easy Breezy Trail once again {10} then continue beneath both the southbound and northbound lanes of SR 179 until you intersect the Bell Rock Pathway {3} at 3.6 miles. Make a left turn onto Bell Rock Pathway then follow it 0.5 mile back to the parking area {1}.

Color Photos: Scan the QR code below for additional color photos of this trail

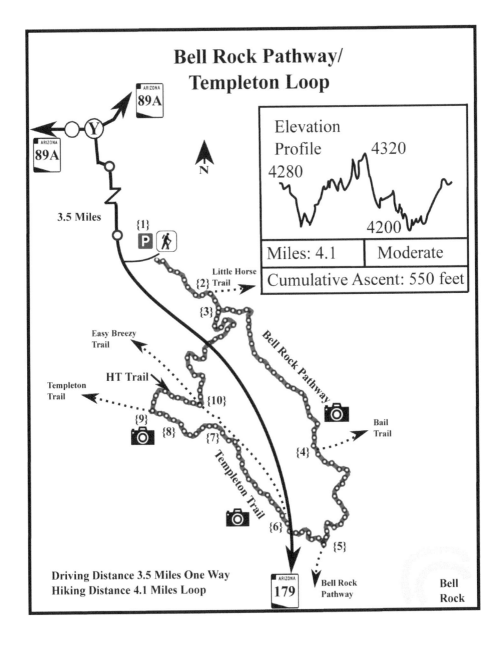

Bell Rock Pathway/
Templeton Loop

89A ARIZONA

89A ARIZONA

3.5 Miles

{1} **P** 🚶

Little Horse Trail
{2}

{3}

Easy Breezy Trail

HT Trail

Templeton Trail

{9}

{8}

{10}

{7}

Bell Rock Pathway

Bail Trail

{4}

Templeton Trail

{6}

{5}

N

Elevation Profile
4280   4320

4200

Miles: 4.1	Moderate
Cumulative Ascent: 550 feet	

Driving Distance 3.5 Miles One Way
Hiking Distance 4.1 Miles Loop

179 ARIZONA

Bell Rock Pathway

Bell Rock

Boynton Canyon and Boynton Vortex ★

Summary: A favorite in-out hike to a famous Sedona vortex area then into a forested canyon with nice red rock views

Challenge Level: Easy for the vortex hike; Moderate for the canyon hike

Hiking Distance: About 0.6 miles each way or 1.2 miles round trip for the vortex; about 3.2 miles each way or 6.4 miles round trip for the canyon hike

Hiking Time: About 1 hour round trip for the vortex; about 3 1/2 hours round trip for the canyon hike

Trail Popularity: 🚶🚶 🚶🚶 🚶🚶 🚶🚶

Trailhead Directions: From the "Y" roundabout (see page 7), drive west toward Cottonwood on SR 89A about 3 miles. Turn right onto Dry Creek Road. Stay on Dry Creek Road to a stop sign (about 3 miles) then turn left onto Boynton Pass Road. Proceed about 1.6 miles to a stop sign. Turn right, the trailhead parking is about 0.1 mile on the right {1}. (34°54.456'N; 111°50.928'W) There are toilets at the parking area.

Description: Boynton Canyon was named for John Boeington who was a horse rancher in the canyon around 1886. Boynton Canyon is a very popular trail. The nicest part of the trail is located beyond the Enchantment Resort. It has summer shade and good red rock views. It is also a well-known vortex site. After hiking about 0.25 mile from the parking area, you'll see a sign for the Boynton Vista Trail to the right {2}. Hike the Vista Trail for about 0.4 mile slightly uphill to two tall rock formations, both of which are considered vortexes {3}. You'll be hiking up about 225 feet to the vortexes. Kachina Woman is to the east; the Warrior is to the west. (Additional information on vortexes can be found on page 6.)

After visiting the vortexes, return to the Boynton Canyon Trail then continue to the north. The trail beside the Enchantment Resort is rocky and narrow, and is the most difficult part of the trail. Once you are past the Enchantment Resort, the trail widens and follows the canyon floor.

Just after you come to the end of the Enchantment Resort property, you can see evidence of prior habitation high up on the right {4}. Soon you'll enter a forest where the trail and views are excellent, although some of the views are blocked by the trees. You'll see some nice fall colors usually during the third or fourth week of October about 2.5 miles from the trailhead. The trail ends in a box canyon after a steep climb at the base of Secret Mountain {5}.

Color Photos: Scan the QR code below for additional color photos of this trail

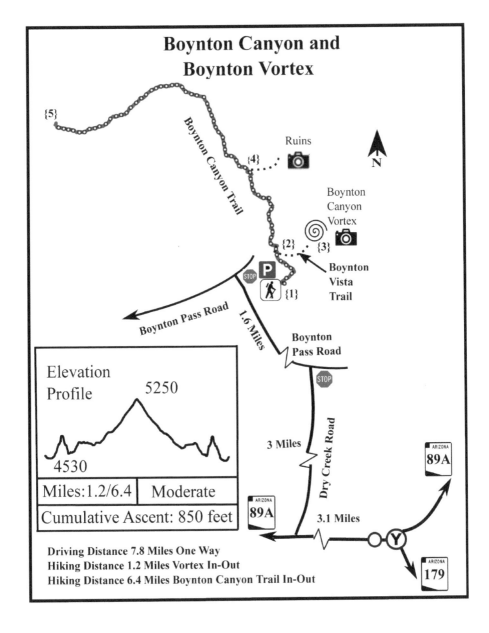

Boynton Canyon and Boynton Vortex

{5}

Boynton Canyon Trail

{4}

Ruins

N

Boynton Canyon Vortex

{2}   {3}

Boynton Vista Trail

STOP   P

{1}

Boynton Pass Road

1.6 Miles

Boynton Pass Road

STOP

3 Miles

Dry Creek Road

ARIZONA 89A

Elevation Profile   5250

4530

Miles: 1.2/6.4 | Moderate

Cumulative Ascent: 850 feet

ARIZONA 89A   3.1 Miles

Driving Distance 7.8 Miles One Way
Hiking Distance 1.2 Miles Vortex In-Out
Hiking Distance 6.4 Miles Boynton Canyon Trail In-Out

ARIZONA 179

Brins Mesa Overlook Trail ★

Summary: A favorite hike up to a beautiful mesa then on to a knoll with red rock views all around.

Challenge Level: Moderate

Hiking Distance: About 1.5 miles each way to the top of Brins Mesa or 3 miles round trip; add 0.7 mile one way to the overlook or 4.4 miles round trip

Hiking Time: About 2 1/2 hours round trip

Trail Popularity:

Trailhead Directions: From the "Y" roundabout (see page 7), drive north on SR 89A about 0.3 mile to the Jordan Road roundabout. Take the third exit onto Jordan Road then drive to the end. Turn left onto West Park Ridge. Drive 0.3 miles then proceed through the paved cul-de-sac, continuing on the dirt road for 0.5 mile to the main parking area {1}. (34°53.287'N; 111°46.098'W) This parking area also serves the Brins Mesa, Cibola, Jim Thompson and Jordan Trails. There are toilets at the parking area. Note: The dirt road is rough with potholes. A high clearance vehicle is recommended.

Description: The trail begins on the west side of the parking area {1}. As you begin the hike up to Brins Mesa, you are rewarded with some outstanding views. You'll be hiking up 1.5 miles and about 550 feet to reach the edge of the mesa. The trail becomes much steeper as you approach it.

Immediately after you reach the mesa {2}, look for a faint trail to your right. You'll follow this trail for 0.2 mile then bear left at a fork in the trail {3}. If you go right, you'll shortly come to a scenic outcropping of red rock, which has a nice view {4}. As you continue along the left fork, the trail continues to gently rise then narrows as it follows the north side of Brins Mesa. You'll soon see the overlook ahead. A moderate amount of scrambling is needed to reach the top of the knoll, but the climb is well worth the effort. Once on top, there is a spectacular view overlooking Mormon Canyon {5}. Look high up on the rock face to the southeast. If you are lucky, that's where you may see Angel Falls flowing with the spring snow melt.

Color Photos: Scan the QR code below for additional color photos of this trail

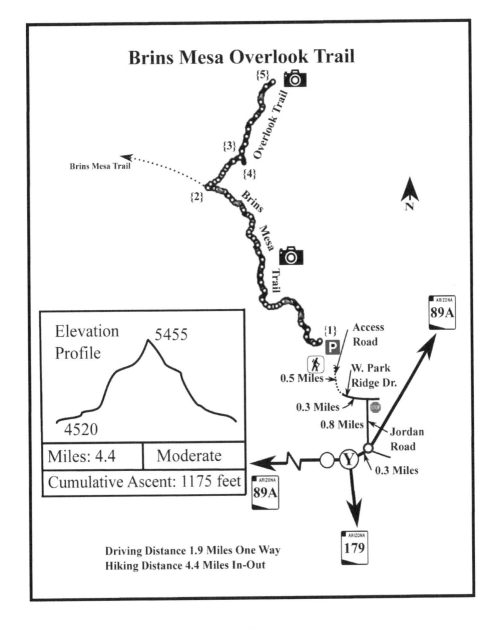

Brins Mesa/Soldier Pass Loop ★

Summary: A favorite loop hike to the top of a beautiful mesa then down past several Sedona landmarks with red rock views all around

Challenge Level: Moderate

Hiking Distance: About 5 miles loop

Hiking Time: About 3 hours round trip

Trail Popularity: 🚶🚶 🚶🚶

Trailhead Directions: From the "Y" roundabout (see page 7), drive north on SR 89A about 0.3 mile to the Jordan Road roundabout. Take the third exit onto Jordan Road then drive to the end. Turn left onto West Park Ridge. Drive 0.3 miles then proceed through the paved cul-de-sac, continuing on the dirt road for 0.5 mile to the main parking area {1}. (34°53.287'N; 111°46.098'W) This parking area also serves the Brins Mesa, Brins Mesa Overlook, Cibola, Jordan and Jim Thompson Trails. There are toilets at the parking area. Note: The dirt road is rough with potholes. A high clearance vehicle is recommended.

Description: You'll actually be hiking 4 trails to complete this loop hike. The Brins Mesa Trail begins on the west side of the parking area {1}. As you begin the hike up to Brins Mesa, you are rewarded with some outstanding views. At 0.6 mile, you'll have a view of Brins Mesa ahead {2}. At 1 mile, you'll cross a fairly large wash {3} then begin a rather steep ascent. Just beyond the wash there is a nice place to stop and take a rest {4}. You'll be hiking up about 550 feet to reach the edge of the mesa {5}. Once you reach the edge of the mesa {5}, you'll enjoy views all around. Continue straight ahead. The trail here is a gentle descent but is very rocky. After hiking about 1 mile, you'll intersect the Soldier Pass Trail {6}. Turn left here.

As you begin the Soldier Pass Trail, there is a nice place to stop and take a break at the 2.3 mile mark {7}. From here, the trail descends rather steeply. At 2.5 miles look to the left for a view of the Soldier Pass Arches {8}. You'll come to a social trail that leads to the arches after 2.8 miles {9} but, be advised, this trail is steep with drop offs so be extremely careful if you attempt to go to the arches. At 2.9 miles, the trail makes a left turn out of a wash {10}.

At 3.6 miles, you'll come to the Seven Sacred Pools, which usually have water in them, even when it hasn't rained for some time {11}. In another 0.3 mile, you'll come to the Devil's Kitchen, a very large sink hole {12}. Continue in an easterly direction then continue onto the Jordan Trail. At 4.3 miles, you'll intersect the Cibola Trail {13}. Continue on the Cibola Trail for another 0.7 mile to return to the parking area where you started.

Color Photos: Scan the QR code below for additional color photos of this trail

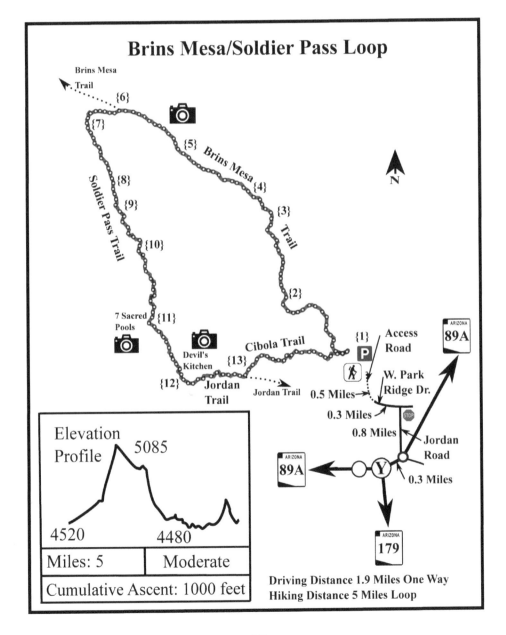

Brins Mesa/Soldier Pass Loop

Brins Mesa
Trail
{6}
{7}
{5}
Brins Mesa
{4}
{3}
{8}
{9}
Soldier Pass Trail
{10}
{2}
7 Sacred Pools {11}
Devil's Kitchen
{13}
Cibola Trail
{1}
Access Road
W. Park Ridge Dr.
{12}
Jordan Trail
Jordan Trail
0.5 Miles
0.3 Miles
0.8 Miles

N

ARIZONA **89A**

ARIZONA **89A**

ARIZONA **179**

Jordan Road
0.3 Miles

Elevation Profile 5085

4520   4480

Miles: 5	Moderate
Cumulative Ascent: 1000 feet	

Driving Distance 1.9 Miles One Way
Hiking Distance 5 Miles Loop

Broken Arrow/Submarine Rock Loop ★

Summary: A favorite sunny, picturesque loop hike to the Devil's Dining Room, Submarine Rock and Chicken Point

Challenge Level: Moderate

Hiking Distance:

About 1.5 miles each way to Chicken Point or 3 miles round trip; about 4 miles round trip if you hike the loop to Submarine Rock then Chicken Point and return

Hiking Time: About 2 1/2 hours round trip

Trail Popularity:

Trailhead Directions: From the "Y" roundabout (see page 7), drive south on SR 179 for 1.5 miles to the roundabout at Morgan Road. Take the third exit then proceed on Morgan Road. Drive about 0.6 mile to the trailhead parking on your left (the last part is a dirt road) {1}. (34°50.738'N; 111°45.424'W) This parking area also serves the Marg's Draw Trail. There is room for about 25 vehicles in the parking area.

Description: The trail is named for the movie, *Broken Arrow,* which was filmed in the area in 1950. From the parking area, go south across the jeep road to the trail. Initially, the trail essentially parallels the jeep road. About 0.2 mile from the parking area, you'll intersect the Hog Wash Trail and in another 75 feet, the Twin Buttes Trail. After hiking about 0.4 mile, watch for a fence on the right which surrounds a large sinkhole known as the Devil's Dining Room {2}. As you continue along the trail, after about another 0.4 mile you'll come to a sign and a fork in the trail {3}. Continue to the right on the Broken Arrow Trail for another 0.7 mile to Chicken Point or turn left to go to Submarine Rock.

Submarine rock is a very large rock formation with panoramic views all around. While you can scramble up on the north end, I prefer to hike around to the south end where it is easy to get on the top of Submarine Rock. To get to Chicken Point from the south end of Submarine Rock, look down and you'll see where the Pink Jeeps park. Go down to that parking area then follow the jeep road southwest to Chicken Point. Be sure to stay out of the way of the jeeps as you hike along this narrow road.

Chicken Point is named for thrill-seeking jeep drivers who once dared to drive close to the edge of the point (jeep access is no longer permitted on Chicken Point). If you look to the south, you'll see a chicken-shaped rock high up on the red rock cliff. Chicken Point is a nice place for a snack break as the views are outstanding {5}. You'll likely encounter some Pink Jeeps as the Broken Arrow tour brings many visitors to this beautiful area.

Color Photos: Scan the QR code below for additional color photos of this trail

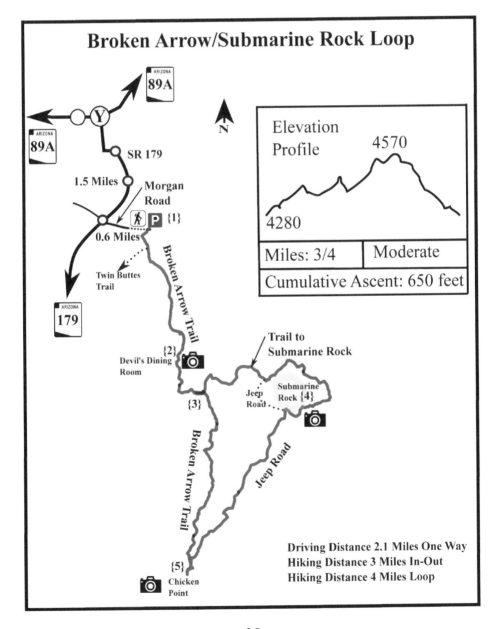

Broken Arrow/Submarine Rock Loop

Elevation Profile
4570
4280

Miles: 3/4	Moderate
Cumulative Ascent: 650 feet	

ARIZONA 89A

ARIZONA 89A

SR 179

1.5 Miles

Morgan Road

{1}

0.6 Miles

Twin Buttes Trail

ARIZONA 179

Broken Arrow Trail

{2}
Devil's Dining Room

Trail to Submarine Rock

{3}

Jeep Road

Submarine Rock {4}

Broken Arrow Trail

Jeep Road

{5}
Chicken Point

Driving Distance 2.1 Miles One Way
Hiking Distance 3 Miles In-Out
Hiking Distance 4 Miles Loop

Cathedral Rock Trail and
Cathedral Vortex Trail ★

Summary: A favorite steep, sunny in-out hike to the saddle of Cathedral Rock for spectacular views all around and the location of one of Sedona's famous vortex sites

Challenge Level: Hard

Hiking Distance: About 0.75 miles each way or 1.5 miles round trip

Hiking Time: About 1 ½ hours round trip

Trail Popularity: 🚶🚶🚶

Trailhead Directions: From the "Y" roundabout (see page 7), drive south on SR 179 about 3.2 miles to the Back O' Beyond roundabout. Take the first exit then go west on the Back O' Beyond Road for about 0.75 mile. The main parking area with 18 spots and the overflow parking area with 22 spots are on your left {1}. (34°49.523'N; 111°47.303'W)

Parking is very limited and fills up fast at this popular trail. Arrive as early as you can. If you are hiking Thursday thru Sunday, you must take the shuttle because the parking area is closed. **(see Trailhead Shuttle Service page 5)** or park at a nearby trailhead (see Baldwin Loop or HT/Easy Breezy Loop) if the parking lot is full.

Description: The first part of the hike is relatively easy – the last part is a steep, strenuous hike. The trail begins on the west side of the main parking area on Back 'O Beyond Road. You'll start out crossing a dry creek bed. Continue climbing up until the trail intersects the Templeton Trail {2}. Turn right then go about 60 paces to the continuation of the Cathedral Rock Trail on your left {3}.

From here, the trail becomes very steep. Hiking boots or other footwear with good traction is recommended. Once you arrive at the saddle of Cathedral Rock {4}, you are at the location of one of four main vortex sites in Sedona. (Additional information on vortexes can be found on page 6.)

There are short trails along the south side of the east and west rock formations that lead to some good views, although the footing can be tricky.

Note: If heights, an extremely steep trail or tenuous footing bothers you, or the trail is wet or snowy (making it slippery), I do not recommend this trail.

Color Photos: Scan the QR code below for additional color photos of this trail

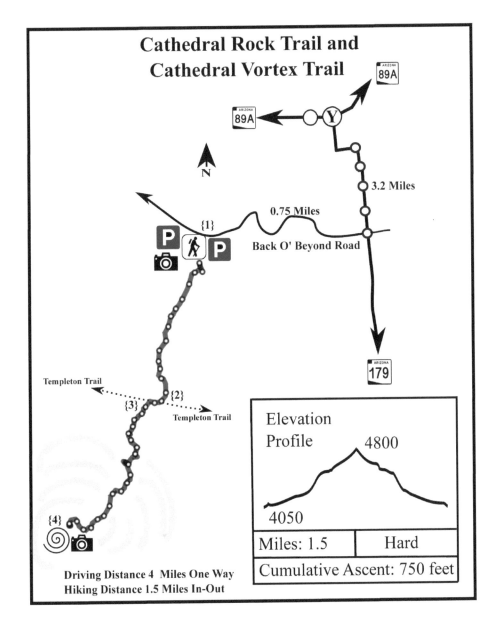

Cathedral Rock Trail and Cathedral Vortex Trail

89A

89A

Y

N

3.2 Miles

0.75 Miles

{1}

P 🚶 P

📷

Back O' Beyond Road

179

Templeton Trail

{3} {2}

Templeton Trail

{4}

📷

Elevation Profile   4800

4050

Miles: 1.5	Hard
Cumulative Ascent: 750 feet	

Driving Distance 4 Miles One Way
Hiking Distance 1.5 Miles In-Out

Chimney Rock Pass Loop ★

Summary: A favorite loop hike around the base of Chimney Rock with panoramic views

Challenge Level: Easy

Hiking Distance: About a 2 mile loop, including overlook

Hiking Time: About 1 1/2 hours round trip

Trail Popularity:

Trailhead Directions: From the "Y" roundabout (see page 7), drive west toward Cottonwood on SR 89A about 3 miles. Turn right onto Dry Creek Road then proceed for 0.5 mile. Turn right onto Thunder Mountain Road then drive 0.7 mile. This parking area is on your left {1}. (34°52.325'N; 111°48.735'W) The entrance gate opens each day at 8:00 am; the exit gate is never closed. The parking area also serves the Chimney Rock Lower Loop and Thunder Mountain/Andante Loop.

Description: From the parking area, go west past the signboard for about 100 feet then turn right onto the Lower Chimney Trail. In 0.1 mile, you'll come to the intersection of the Thunder Mountain and Lower Chimney Trails {2}.

For a morning hike, turn right here onto the Thunder Mountain Trail to hike in a counterclockwise direction because the views are better with the sun at your back. For an afternoon hike, continue straight ahead on the Lower Chimney Trail to hike in a clockwise direction.

As you circle Chimney Rock in the counterclockwise direction, you'll soon see a large water tank on the right, and intersect a social trail after 0.4 mile {3}. Next you'll intersect the Andante Trail {4}. After 0.7 mile, the Thunder Mountain Trail goes off to the right {5}. Turn left here onto the Chimney Rock Pass Trail.

In 0.2 mile, look for a faint trail off to the right which leads to a scenic overlook {6}. You'll hike around the base of the first rock outcropping then scramble up on the second rock outcropping for the scenic view {7}; it's a 0.3 mile in-out scramble but worth it for the view.

About 125 feet past the trail to the overlook is another unmarked trail {8} to the left and another scramble, which leads to the base of the chimney of Chimney Rock. As you continue on, you'll intersect the Lizard Head Trail on the right {9} and an unmarked social trail {10} where you should bear left. At 1.4 miles, you'll intersect a sign for the Lower Chimney Rock Trail and Summit, which is the summit on Little Sugarloaf {11}; stay left to complete the Chimney Rock Loop.

Note: The signage on the trail shows Chimney Rock Trail and Chimney Rock Pass Trail at various places between {8} and {2}. Don't worry, you are on the correct trail. This trail is a favorite for local residents so you'll likely encounter people walking their dogs.

Color Photos: Scan the QR code below for additional color photos of this trail

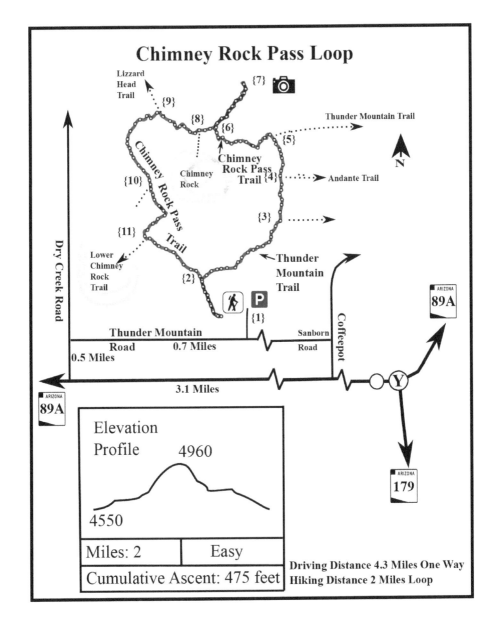

Chimney Rock Pass Loop

Lizzard Head Trail

{9}

{8}

{7}

{6}

Thunder Mountain Trail

{5}

N

Chimney Rock Pass Trail {4}

Chimney Rock

Andante Trail

{10}

{3}

{11}

Lower Chimney Rock Trail

Thunder Mountain Trail

{2}

{1}

Dry Creek Road

Thunder Mountain Road 0.7 Miles

0.5 Miles

Sanborn Road

Coffeepot

ARIZONA 89A

3.1 Miles

ARIZONA 89A

Y

ARIZONA 179

Elevation Profile 4960

4550

Miles: 2	Easy
Cumulative Ascent: 475 feet	

Driving Distance 4.3 Miles One Way
Hiking Distance 2 Miles Loop

Chuckwagon Loop

Summary: A pleasant loop hike on a former mountain bike trail that parallels Forest Road 152 then goes to Long Canyon Road with partial shade, good red rock views all around and is an alternative way to get to the Devil's Bridge Trail

Challenge Level: Moderate

Hiking Distance: About 4.7 mile loop from the Mescal Day Use Trailhead parking area

Hiking Time: About 3 hours round trip from the Mescal Day Use Trailhead parking area

Trail Popularity: 🚶🚶🚶

Trailhead Directions: From the "Y" roundabout (see page 7), drive west toward Cottonwood on SR 89A about 3 miles. Turn right onto Dry Creek Road. Stay on Dry Creek Road to a stop sign (about 3 miles) then turn right onto Long Canyon Road. Drive 0.3 mile to the Mescal Day Use Trailhead parking area on the left {1} (34°54.100'N; 111°49.667'W) or right {2} Parking is very limited at this parking area. Rather than attempting to park at the parking lot, a better choice is to take the shuttle **(see Trailhead Shuttle Service page 5)** if the parking lot is full.

Description: I suggest hiking this loop from the Mescal Day Use Trailhead parking area {1} {2}. Look for a sign that points south to the Chuckwagon Trail at the northeast end of t parking area {2}. Hike this connector trail south 0.25 mile to the intersection with the Chuckwagon Trail {3} then turn left. You'll soon have some very nice panoramic views to the north {4}.

Hike northeast for 0.8 mile from {4} to a sign To Devils Bridge {4} which will lead you to the Devil's Bridge parking area {6} (see the Devil's Bridge Trail). There is a nice spot for a snack 0.15 mile past the turn to Devil's Bridge {7}. As you continue, you'll have views on both sides. The trail continues with a series of ups and downs, but nothing too steep. After about 2 additional miles, you'll come to a fork in the trail {8}. The right fork leads to Brins Mesa trailhead after 0.5 mile. The Chuckwagon Trail continues to the left.

You'll cross a shallow wash then a deeper wash after 0.2 mile {9}. There is a nice spot to stop after another 0.6 mile {10}. The trail takes two sharp turns then is relatively flat for the next 0.6 mile until you come to Long Canyon Road {11}. Cross the road and continue just past the interpretive signboard then turn left onto the connector trail. Follow the connector trail to the intersection with the Mescal Trail {12} Turn left here then follow the Mescal Trail back to the parking area {1} {2}.

Note: You'll likely encounter mountain bikers as this is a favorite bike trail. Also, for a longer hike start at the Dry Creek parking area {12}. This will add 2.2 miles to the hike for a total of 6.9 miles.

Color Photos: Scan the QR code below for additional color photos of this trail

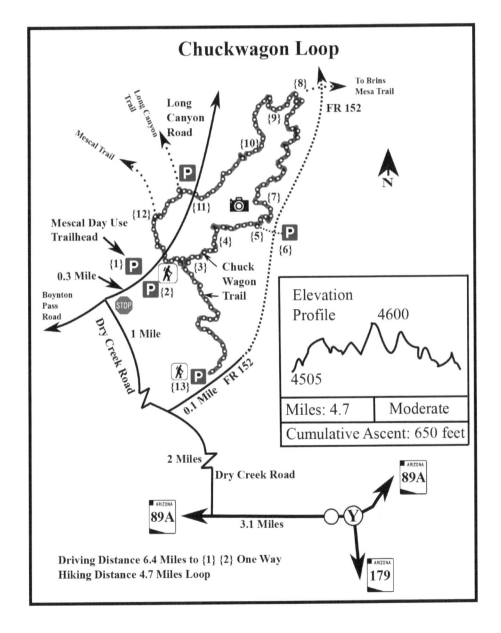

Cibola Pass/Jordan Loop

Summary:
This close-to-town loop hike provides some spectacular red rock views with the option to visit the Devil's Kitchen sinkhole and the Seven Sacred Pools

Challenge Level:
Easy to Moderate

Hiking Distance:
About 0.75 mile each way or 1.5 miles round trip; about a 2.2 mile loop if you hike the Cibola Pass Trail then return on the Jordan Trail; about 3.6 miles loop if you hike the Cibola Pass Trail to the Jordan Trail to the Soldier Pass Trail to the Seven Sacred Pools returning via the Jordan Trail

Hiking Time: About 1 ½ hour round trip for the Cibola Pass/Jordan loop; about 2 ½ hours round trip to the Seven Sacred Pools and return

Trail Popularity: 🚶🚶 🚶🚶 🚶

Trailhead Directions: From the "Y" roundabout (see page 7), drive north on SR 89A about 0.3 mile to the Jordan Road roundabout. Take the third exit onto Jordan Road then drive to the end. Turn left onto West Park Ridge. Drive 0.3 miles then proceed through the paved cul-de-sac, continuing on the dirt road for 0.5 mile to the main parking area {1}. (34°53.287'N; 111°46.098'W) This parking area also serves the Brins Mesa, Brins Mesa Overlook, Jim Thompson and Jordan Trails. There are toilets at the parking area. Note: The dirt road is rough with potholes. A high clearance vehicle is recommended.

Description: Begin hiking the trail on the west side of the parking area near the toilets. Go through the opening in the cable fence. The Cibola Pass Trail branches left from the Brins Mesa Trail after about 400 feet {2}. The trail is quite steep in places. As you proceed, you'll have some very nice red rock views including the Cibola Mitten rock formation. At about 0.4 mile, you'll approach two fence posts on the left side {3}. If you go straight for a short distance, you'll have some great views. Return to the fence posts then continue on the trail. You'll intersect the Jordan Trail after hiking 0.75 mile {4}. Turn around here to return to the parking area via the Cibola Trail for a 1.5 mile hike Or turn south and follow the Jordan Trail back to the parking area for a 2.2 mile loop.

Or proceed west on the Jordan Trail for 0.4 mile to the Soldier Pass Trail. Turn right onto the Soldier Pass Trail, which leads to Devil's Kitchen (a very large sink hole) {5}. Continue on the Soldier Pass Trail for 0.4 mile and you'll arrive at the Seven Sacred Pools {6}. You'll have hiked about 3.6 miles for the entire hike from the Seven Sacred Pools when you return to the parking area via the Jordan Trail.

Color Photos: Scan the QR code below for additional color photos of this trail

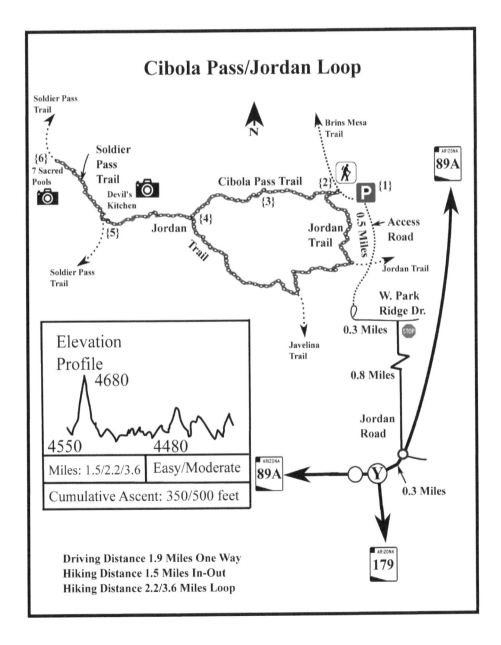

Cibola Pass/Jordan Loop

Courthouse Butte Loop

Summary: A pleasant loop hike circling Bell Rock and Courthouse Butte

Challenge Level: Moderate

Hiking Distance: About 4.2 miles loop

Hiking Time: About 2 ½ hours round trip

Trail Popularity:

Trailhead Directions: There are two parking areas you can use for this hike. There are toilets at both the parking areas. From the "Y" roundabout (see page 7), drive south on SR 179 for about 5 miles to the first parking area. After you drive about 3.2 miles, just past the Back O' Beyond roundabout, SR 179 becomes a divided highway. Continue driving south. About 1.8 miles beyond the Back O' Beyond roundabout, southbound SR 179 adds a passing lane on the left. From the passing lane, turn left at the sign for the Court House Vista parking area {1}. (34°48.350'N; 111°46.009'W)

Before you turn, you'll see Bell Rock ahead of you on the left side of SR 179. The trail starts on the southeast side of the parking area. After you park, walk past the interpretive signboard then proceed straight ahead on the Bell Rock Trail. Follow it for 0.1 mile to the intersection with the Courthouse Butte Loop Trail {2}.

If you continue driving south on SR 179, in 1 mile you'll come to the Bell Rock Vista parking area south of Bell Rock on your left. Turn left into the parking area {8}. (34°47.501'N; 111°45.699'W) Follow the Bell Rock Pathway Trail north for about 0.5 mile until you intersect the Courthouse Butte Loop Trail {7}.

Description: These trails circling Courthouse Butte and Bell Rock combine panoramic and close-up views of these two famous rock formations as well as distant views of Rabbit Ears, the Chapel of the Holy Cross and Cathedral Rock. The trail is fairly open, so it provides limited shade making it a hot summer hike.

I like to hike this loop in the clockwise direction from the Bell Rock Vista parking area {8}, although either direction provides great views. From the Bell Rock Vista parking area, the trail starts out wide and is defined by fences on both sides. Follow the Bell Rock Pathway around the west side of Bell Rock then follow the signs for Courthouse Butte Loop between {2} and {3}. You'll intersect several trails as you hike including the Llama Trail {3} and Big Park Loop Trail {5} {6}. A good stopping point for a snack break is near Muffin Rock, which some call UFO Rock {4}. The Courthouse Butte Loop Trail and the Big Park Loop Trail are combined between {5} and {6}. For a shortcut back to the parking lot, turn left at {6} where you'll see a sign pointing to the Big Park Loop Trail.

Color Photos: Scan the QR code below for additional color photos of this trail

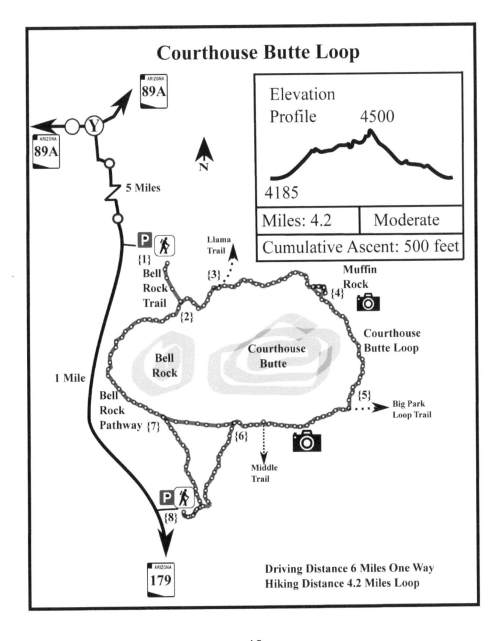

Courthouse Butte Loop

ARIZONA **89A**

ARIZONA **89A**

Y

5 Miles

N

Elevation Profile   4500

4185

Miles: 4.2	Moderate
Cumulative Ascent: 500 feet	

P 🚶 {1}

Llama Trail

{3}

Muffin Rock {4} 📷

Bell Rock Trail

{2}

Courthouse Butte Loop

1 Mile

Bell Rock

Courthouse Butte

Bell Rock Pathway {7}

{5} ➔ Big Park Loop Trail

{6}

📷

Middle Trail

P 🚶 {8}

ARIZONA **179**

Driving Distance 6 Miles One Way
Hiking Distance 4.2 Miles Loop

Devil's Bridge Trail ★

Summary: A favorite in-out climb with steep stairs up to the largest natural stone arch in the Sedona area

Challenge Level: Moderate

Hiking Distance: About 3.1 miles each way from the Dry Creek Vista parking area or 6.2 miles round trip; about 1 mile each way From the Devil's Bridge (DB) parking area or 2 miles round trip; about 2.2 miles each way from the Mescal Trail parking area or 4.4 miles round trip;

Hiking Time: About 3 ½ hours round trip from the Dry Creek Vista parking area; about 1½ hour round trip from the DB parking area; about 2 ½ hours round trip from the Mescal Day Use Trailhead parking area

Trail Popularity: 🚶🚶🚶🚶

Trailhead Directions: From the "Y" roundabout (see page 7), drive west toward Cottonwood on SR 89A about 3 miles. Turn right onto Dry Creek Road. Stay on Dry Creek Road for about 2 miles then turn right onto Forest Road (FR) 152. Drive for 0.2 mile and park at the Dry Creek Vista parking area on the left {1}. (34° 53.425'N; 111°49.240'W) If you have a high clearance vehicle, proceed for another 1.1 miles on the unpaved, very rough FR 152 to the DB parking area on your right {2}. (34°54.172'N; 111°48.833'W) Or rather than turn onto FR 152, a third alternative is to continue on Dry Creek Road another 1 mile to a stop sign then turn right onto Long Canyon Road. Drive 0.3 mile to the Mescal Day Use Trailhead parking area on the left {3} (34°54.100'N; 111°49.667'W) or right {4}. Parking is very limited at these parking areas. Rather than attempting to park at the parking lots, a better choice is to take the shuttle **(see Trailhead Shuttle Service page 5)** if the parking lots are full.

Note: FR 152 is an extremely rough road beyond the 0.2 mile paved section; a high clearance vehicle and 4WD are strongly recommended.

Description: From the Dry Creek Vista parking area {1}, go to the signboard where you'll see a small sign pointing to the right for the Chuckwagon (CW) Trail. Follow the CW Trail and after 0.7 mile, you'll come to a fork and a signpost {5}. The right fork leads to FR 152. I recommend that you continue on the CW Trail otherwise you'll be hiking on the dusty FR 152 road. You'll pass the intersection of the trail to the Mescal Day Use Trailhead parking area {3} {4} after 1.1 miles {6}. Continue on the CW Trail for a total of 2.1 miles then turn right onto the connector trail {7} to the Devil's Bridge parking area across FR 152 {2}.

For most folks, I recommend starting from the Mescal Day Use Trailhead parking area {3} {4}. Hike the connector trail from the northeast end of parking area {4} for 0.2 mile then turn left onto the CW Trail {6}. Hike for 0.8 mile to the turn to Devil's Bridge {7}.

Devil's Bridge is a large natural stone arch that you can walk on. It is reachable with a moderate amount of climbing (up some 400 feet); the view of the arch and from the arch are well worth the climb. The trail splits about 15 feet past a large rock next to the trail {8}. Go straight then right to reach the top of the arch; take the left fork to go beneath the arch. If you take the trail to the top of the arch {9}, you'll be hiking up some steep natural stone steps (with no hand rails) so watch your footing. If you have a fear of heights, you may want to be extra careful on this hike, or only take the left trail to view the arch from beneath. Devil's Bridge gets very busy on weekends and holidays.

Color Photos: Scan the QR code below or additional color photos of this trail

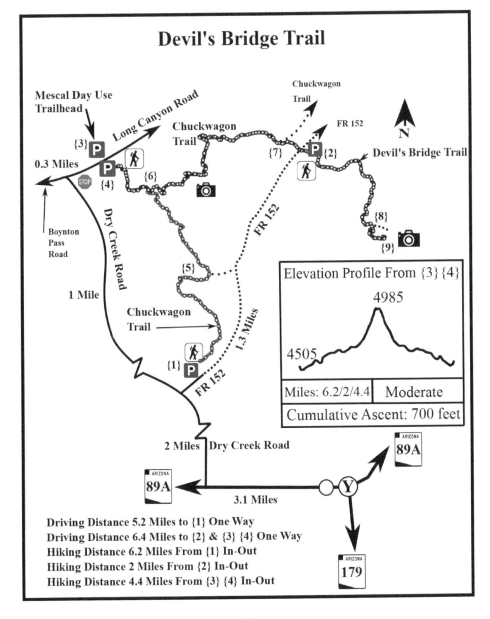

Devil's Bridge Trail

Mescal Day Use Trailhead

Long Canyon Road

Chuckwagon Trail

Chuckwagon Trail

{3}
0.3 Miles
{4}
{6}

{7}

FR 152

{2}

Devil's Bridge Trail

Boynton Pass Road

Dry Creek Road

FR 152

{8}

{9}

1 Mile

{5}

Chuckwagon Trail

1.3 Miles

{1}

FR 152

Elevation Profile From {3} {4}

4985

4505

Miles: 6.2/2/4.4 | Moderate

Cumulative Ascent: 700 feet

2 Miles | Dry Creek Road

ARIZONA 89A

89A

3.1 Miles

Y

ARIZONA 179

Driving Distance 5.2 Miles to {1} One Way
Driving Distance 6.4 Miles to {2} & {3} {4} One Way
Hiking Distance 6.2 Miles From {1} In-Out
Hiking Distance 2 Miles From {2} In-Out
Hiking Distance 4.4 Miles From {3} {4} In-Out

Doe Mountain Trail ★

Summary: A favorite climb up to the top of Doe Mountain with panoramic red rock views all around

Challenge Level: Moderate

Hiking Distance:
About 2.6 miles loop

Hiking Time:
About 2 hours round trip

Trail Popularity: 🚶🚶🚶

Trailhead Directions: From the "Y" roundabout (see page 7), drive west toward Cottonwood on SR 89A about 3 miles. Turn right onto Dry Creek Road. Stay on Dry Creek Road to a stop sign (about 3 miles) then turn left onto Boynton Pass Road. Proceed about 1.6 miles to a stop sign. Turn left, continuing on Boynton Pass Road. The trailhead parking is the second one on the left side, about 1.8 miles from the stop sign {1}. (34°53.596'N; 111°51.945'W) The trailhead is at the south side of the parking area. This parking area also serves the Bear Mountain Trail. There are toilets at the parking area.

Description: From the parking area, hike southeast toward Doe Mountain and you'll soon intersect the Aerie Trail {2}. The trail has several switchbacks and is narrow in places. Just before you reach the rim, you'll hike up a narrow slot in the rocks. Once through the slot and on the mesa, turn around and look down at the parking area. Pay attention to where you came up {3} by observing your location relative to the parking area below because it can be hard to find the way back down after hiking around the top of Doe Mountain.

Although the top of Doe Mountain is crisscrossed with social trails, the preferred way is to proceed straight across to the southern side of Doe Mountain then proceed in a clockwise direction around then back to the trail down to the parking area. Another popular way is to go to the left then skirt the outer edge of the mountain for some great views {4}{5}{6}{7}. You may be bushwhacking a bit, so be sure to wear hiking boots to protect your ankles from the cactus and brush you'll be stepping over. The spectacular views are all around.

Note: The unmarked, unmaintained trail is difficult to follow at times. I strongly recommend using a portable GPS unit to hike around the top of Doe Mountain and back to the trail to the parking area (go to https://greatsedonahikes.com/gps/gps.html).

Color Photos: Scan the QR code below for additional color photos of this trail

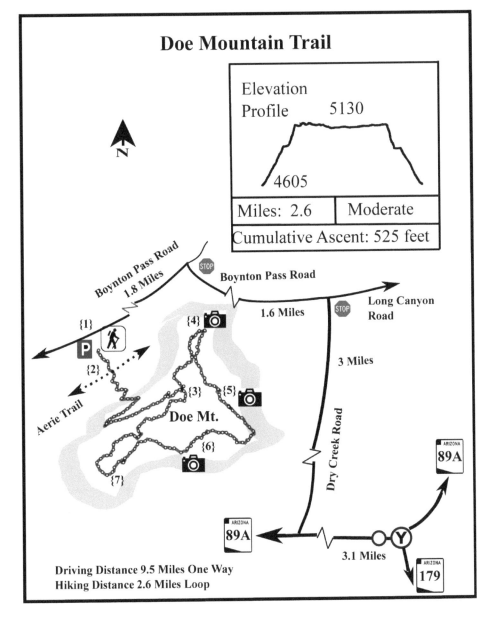

Doe Mountain Trail

Elevation Profile 5130

4605

| Miles: 2.6 | Moderate |

Cumulative Ascent: 525 feet

N

Boynton Pass Road
1.8 Miles

STOP Boynton Pass Road

Long Canyon Road

1.6 Miles STOP

{1}

P

{4}

{2}

3 Miles

Aerie Trail

{3} {5}

Doe Mt.

{6}

Dry Creek Road

{7}

ARIZONA 89A

ARIZONA 89A

3.1 Miles

Y

ARIZONA 179

Driving Distance 9.5 Miles One Way
Hiking Distance 2.6 Miles Loop

Fay Canyon Trail ★

Summary: A favorite short, pleasant in-out stroll through a canyon with wonderful red rock views and an optional side trip to view a natural arch

Challenge Level:
Easy for the Fay Canyon Trail; Moderate if you climb up to Fay Canyon Arch

Hiking Distance:
About 1.2 miles each way to the rock slide or 2.4 miles round trip. Add 0.5 mile round trip if you hike to Fay Canyon Arch or 2.9 miles round trip.

Hiking Time:
About 1 ½ hours round trip

Trail Popularity:
🚶🚶 🚶🚶 🚶🚶 🚶🚶

Trailhead Directions:
From the "Y" roundabout (see page 7), drive west toward Cottonwood on SR 89A about 3 miles. Turn right onto Dry Creek Road. Stay on Dry Creek Road to a stop sign (about 3 miles) then turn left onto Boynton Pass Road. Proceed about 1.6 miles to a stop sign. Turn left, continuing on Boynton Pass Road. Park at the first parking area on the left side, about 0.8 miles from the stop sign {1}. (34°54.101'N; 111°51.450'W) The trailhead is across the road from the west end of the parking area. There are toilets at the parking area.

Description: Fay Canyon is one of my favorite trails for non-hiker guests because it is short, relatively level, and very scenic. The trail essentially ends at a massive rock slide {4}.

For those wanting a greater challenge, there is a side trail {2} located on the east side of the main trail about 0.6 mile from the main parking area that leads to a natural stone arch {3}. (See photo above) The arch is somewhat obscured by the trees. You'll have to scramble up about 225 feet on this unmarked trail if you want to go to the arch, which is located up next to the cliff face {3}. This will add about 0.5 mile to the hike. This side trail is narrow and steep with cactus along the edges and loose rock so watch your footing. There is a narrow slot up under the arch where the rocks have separated and you can slip into the opening. Some people suggest that the area under the arch is a powerful vortex spot. (Additional information on vortexes can be found on page 6.)

Color Photos: Scan the QR code below for additional color photos of this trail

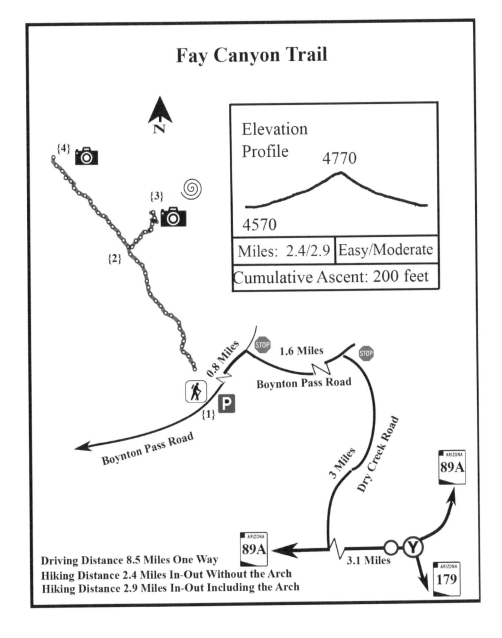

Fay Canyon Trail

N

{4}

{3}

{2}

{1}

Elevation Profile

4770

4570

Miles: 2.4/2.9 | Easy/Moderate

Cumulative Ascent: 200 feet

0.8 Miles

STOP

1.6 Miles

STOP

Boynton Pass Road

P

Boynton Pass Road

3 Miles

Dry Creek Road

ARIZONA 89A

Driving Distance 8.5 Miles One Way
Hiking Distance 2.4 Miles In-Out Without the Arch
Hiking Distance 2.9 Miles In-Out Including the Arch

ARIZONA 89A

3.1 Miles

Y

ARIZONA 179

HiLine Trail ★

Summary: A favorite in-out or two-vehicle hike on a narrow trail that skirts the face of a red rock formation offering panoramic views of Sedona's red rocks.

Challenge Level: Moderate

Hiking Distance: 2 miles each way to a great view of Cathedral Rock or 4 miles round trip; about 3.6 miles each way to the Baldwin Loop Trail or 7.2 miles round trip; 4.7 miles as a two-vehicle hike from the Yavapai Vista parking area to the Turkey Creek parking area

Hiking Time: About 2 hours to the great view of Cathedral Rock round trip; about 4 hours to the Baldwin Trail and return; about 3 hours as a two vehicle hike to the Turkey Creek parking area from the Yavapai Vista parking area

Trail Popularity: 🚶🚶

Trailhead Directions: From the "Y" roundabout (see page 7), drive south on SR 179 about 4.8 miles to mile marker 308.5 then turn right into the Yavapai Vista parking area {1}. (34°48.442'N: 111°46.174'W) (Note: The Yavapai Vista parking area is accessible only from southbound SR 179.) For a two-vehicle hike, park the second vehicle at the Turkey Creek Trail parking area {14}, located 4 miles west on Verde Valley School Road (see Baldwin Loop). (34°48.762'N; 111°48.589'W)

Description: Hike past the interpretive signboard and around the metal railing then continue straight ahead. At the intersection of the Kaibab and Yavapai Vista Trails {2}, continue on the Kaibab Trail for 0.2 mile then turn left onto the Slim Shady Trail {3}. There are no signs for the HiLine Trail at this point. Continue on Slim Shady for about 0.2 mile where you will see a sign and the beginning of the HiLine Trail on your right {4}.

The HiLine Trail is used by many mountain bikers so you may encounter them on this narrow trail. The trail has a number of narrow spots {5} so watch your footing. You'll have nice views of Courthouse Butte, Bell Rock, Lee Mountain, Rabbit Ears, and get your first view of Cathedral Rock after 1.2 miles from the parking area {6}. As you continue, the views of Cathedral Rock get better and better {7}. A good place to stop is 2 miles from the parking area {8}. I suggest you turn around here for a 4 mile round trip hike, but if you wish to hike further, make a right turn to begin the descent. You'll intersect the Transept Trail and after 0.4 mile the trail turns west at a cairn {9} You'll be crossing large expanses of slick rock for the next 0.6 mile. At 3 miles from the parking area, the trail begins a steep, slippery descent so watch your footing {10}. Shortly after the descent you'll be in a wash and as you continue you'll intersect the Baldwin Loop Trail in another 0.6 mile {11}. Turn around here for a 7.2 mile round trip hike, or, for a two vehicle hike, turn left onto the Baldwin Trail, follow it for 0.6 mile then turn left (south) at the sign {12} for the trail to the Turkey Creek parking area {14}. In 400 feet, bear right {13} for a shortcut back to the Turkey Creek parking area {14}.

Note: This trail is narrow and uneven with large drop-offs – do not attempt it if there is snow or ice on the trail.

Color Photos: Scan the QR code below for additional color photos of this trail

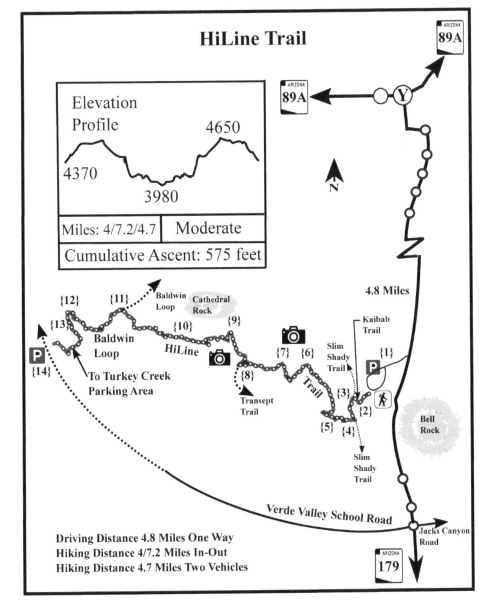

Little Horse Trail ★

Summary:
A favorite in-out hike to Chicken Point, a large slick rock knoll with majestic views

Challenge Level: Moderate

Hiking Distance:
About 2 miles each way or 4 miles round trip

Hiking Time:
About 2 hours round trip

Trail Popularity: 🚶🚶🚶🚶

Trailhead Directions: From the "Y" roundabout (see page 7), drive south on SR 179 about 3.5 miles. Just past the Back O' Beyond roundabout, you'll see a Scenic View sign and a hiking sign on the right side of SR 179 and a left turn lane on the left. Turn left here then proceed to the parking area {1}. (34°49.433'N; 111°46.555'W) The parking area also serves the Bell Rock Pathway/Templeton Loop and HT/Easy Breezy Loop. There are toilets at the parking area. Parking is limited at these popular trails. Rather than attempting to park at the trailhead, a better choice is to take the shuttle **(see Trailhead Shuttle Service page 5)** if the parking area is full.

Description: You'll begin by hiking south on the Bell Rock Pathway for 0.3 mile until it intersects the beginning of the Little Horse Trail {2}. Turn left here onto the Little Horse Trail. When you come to a deep dry wash, go to the left in the wash then follow the trail east then north toward the Twin Buttes, an impressive red rock formation.

After about 1 mile, you'll intersect the Llama Trail on the right {3}. You will intersect the Chapel Trail at the 1.5 mile mark {4}. If you have the time, follow the Chapel Trail for 0.6 mile until it intersects Chapel Road and go up to visit the Chapel of the Holy Cross {5}.

Returning to the Little Horse Trail, continue on for another 0.5 mile where you'll arrive at an expansive area of slick rock known as Chicken Point. The climb up to Chicken Point isn't hard and is well worth the effort {6}.

Chicken Point is named for thrill-seeking jeep drivers who once dared to drive close to the edge of the point (jeep access is no longer permitted on Chicken Point). If you look to the south, you'll see a chicken-shaped rock high up on the red rock cliff. Chicken Point is a nice place for a snack break as the views are outstanding. You'll likely encounter some Pink Jeeps as the Broken Arrow tour brings many visitors to this beautiful area.

Color Photos: Scan the QR code below for additional color photos of this trail

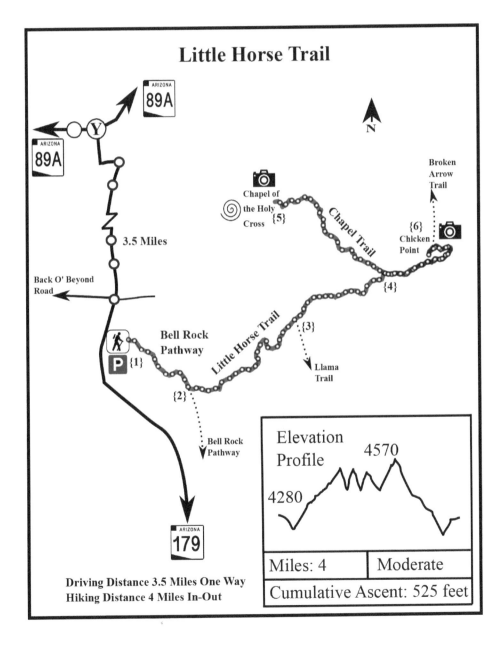

Little Horse Trail

ARIZONA 89A

ARIZONA 89A

Y

N

3.5 Miles

Back O' Beyond Road

Chapel of the Holy Cross {5}

Chapel Trail

Broken Arrow Trail

{6} Chicken Point

{4}

Bell Rock Pathway {1}

Little Horse Trail

{3}

Llama Trail

{2}

Bell Rock Pathway

Elevation Profile

4570

4280

Miles: 4	Moderate
Cumulative Ascent: 525 feet	

ARIZONA 179

Driving Distance 3.5 Miles One Way
Hiking Distance 4 Miles In-Out

Llama/Bail Loop or Llama/Little Horse Loop

Summary: A loop hike with panoramic views of many of Sedona's famous rock formations

Challenge Level:
Easy to Moderate

Hiking Distance: About 4.4 miles for the Llama/ Bail/Bell Rock Pathway loop; about 6 miles for the Llama/ Little Horse/Bell Rock Pathway/Phone Trail loop

Hiking Time: About 2 ¼ hours for the Llama/Bail Loop; about 3 hours round trip for the Llama/Little Horse/Bell Rock Pathway/Phone Trail Loop;

Trail Popularity: 🚶🚶 🚶🚶 🚶🚶

Trailhead Directions: From the "Y" roundabout (see page 7), drive south on SR 179 for about 5 miles to the parking area. After you drive about 3.2 miles, just past the Back O' Beyond roundabout, SR 179 becomes a divided highway. Continue driving south. About 1.8 miles beyond the Back O' Beyond roundabout, southbound SR 179 adds a passing lane on the left. From the passing lane, turn left at the sign for the Court House Vista parking area {1}. This parking area also serves the Bell Rock Climb, Bell Rock Loop, and Courthouse Butte Loop Trails. (34°48.350'N; 111°46.009'W) Before you turn, you'll see Bell Rock ahead of you on the left side of SR 179. This parking area also serves the Bell Rock Climb, Bell Rock Loop, and Courthouse Butte Loop Trails. There are toilets at the parking area. The trail starts on the southeast side of the parking area. There is another Llama trailhead off of the Little Horse Trail {8}. Parking is limited at Little Horse Trail parking area. Rather than attempting to park here, a better choice is to take the shuttle **(see Trailhead Shuttle Service page 5)** if the parking area is full.

Description: The Llama Trail goes from Bell Rock to the Little Horse Trail. It is a favorite of mountain bikers. From the parking area, proceed past the interpretive signboard then follow the Bell Rock Trail 0.1 mile to the intersection with the Bell Rock Pathway {2}. Turn left (northeast) at the sign that says, To Courthouse Butte Loop then follow the Bell Rock Pathway 0.3 mile. Continue straight ahead onto the Courthouse Butte Loop Trail {3}. Follow Courthouse Butte Loop for about 300 feet then turn left onto the Llama Trail {4}.

In 1 mile, you'll come to a scenic area with 8 depressions in the slick rock that are usually filled with water {5}. Continue another 0.9 mile to the intersection with the Bail Trail {6}. You can turn left here then follow the Bail Trail 0.4 mile to the intersection with the Bell Rock Pathway {7}, or proceed another 1.1 miles on the Llama Trail to the Little Horse Trail {8} then turn left to reach the Bell Rock Pathway {9}. Hike south on the Bell Rock Pathway then turn onto the Phone Trail {10} for a shortcut back to the parking area. The Llama Trail approaches Lee Mountain and provides outstanding views of Bell Rock, Courthouse Butte, Twin Buttes and Cathedral Rock. There isn't much shade on this trail so it would be a good choice in cooler weather.

Color Photos: Scan the QR code below for additional color photos of this trail

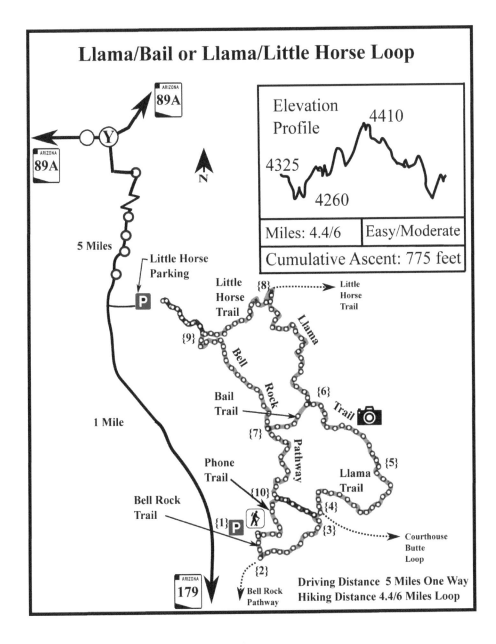

Llama/Bail or Llama/Little Horse Loop

Elevation Profile

4410

4325

4260

Miles: 4.4/6	Easy/Moderate
Cumulative Ascent: 775 feet	

Little Horse Parking

Little Horse Trail

{8}

Little Horse Trail

Llama

{9}

Bell

Rock

{6}

Bail Trail

Trail

{7}

Pathway

Llama Trail

{5}

Phone Trail

{10}

{4}

Bell Rock Trail

{1}

{3}

Courthouse Butte Loop

{2}

Bell Rock Pathway

Driving Distance 5 Miles One Way
Hiking Distance 4.4/6 Miles Loop

ARIZONA 89A

ARIZONA 89A

5 Miles

1 Mile

ARIZONA 179

Mescal/Long Canyon Loop ★

Summary: A favorite in-out hike that skirts the base of Mescal Mountain with both panoramic and up close red rock views with the option for a loop hike

Challenge Level: Easy to Moderate

Hiking Distance: About 2.4 miles each way to the Deadman's Pass Trail intersection or 4.8 miles round trip; about 5 miles for Mescal Trail to Deadman's Pass Trail to Long Canyon Trail loop

Hiking Time: About 2 ½ hours for the in-out hike to Deadman's Pass Trail round trip; about 3 hours for the Mescal/Long Canyon loop round trip

Trail Popularity: 🚶🚶🚶

Trailhead Directions: From the "Y" roundabout (see page 7), drive west toward Cottonwood on SR 89A about 3 miles. Turn right onto Dry Creek Road. Stay on Dry Creek Road to a stop sign (about 3 miles) then turn right onto Long Canyon Road. Proceed 0.3 mile to the Mescal Day Use Trailhead parking area on the left on the left {1} (34°54.100'N; 111°49.667'W) or on the right {2}. There are toilets and picnic tables here. These parking areas also serve the Devil's Bridge and Chuck Wagon Trails. The trail begins near the signboard in parking area {1} or across the road from parking area {2}.

Description: This is a favorite trail that provides both close-up and distant red rock views. After the first 0.1 mile, the trail begins to gently rise as you approach the base of Mescal Mountain. At 0.25 mile, you'll intersect the connector trail to Long Canyon Trail on your right {3}. Continue straight ahead. At 0.4 mile, you are on the top of a high bluff with good red rock views all around. You'll pass a cairn and trail marker for the Yucca Trail {4} then at the 1 mile mark, look up high to the right where you'll observe a large cave in the side of Mescal Mountain {5}. Soon the trail becomes very narrow in places with steep drop offs – watch your footing. You'll find signs indicating difficult and extreme portions of the trail for the mountain bikers. I recommend you hike the difficult path. After 1.75 miles, you'll come to a cairn and trail marker for the Canyon of Fools Trail [6]. Just beyond you can see Kachina Woman and the Warrior in Boynton Canyon, Cockscomb, Doe Mountain, Bear Mountain and Courthouse Butte in the distance.

As you proceed, the views get better and better. At 2.2 miles [7], the trail begins to descend some 85 feet in 0.25 mile and intersects the Deadman's Pass Trail [8]. Turn around here or, if you wish to hike a loop, turn right onto the Deadman's Pass Trail then hike for 0.9 mile to the Long Canyon Trail. Turn right onto the Long Canyon Trail {9} then follow it back toward Long Canyon Road. You'll see a connector trail just before the parking area on Long Canyon Road {10}. Turn right to follow the connector trail back to the Mescal Trail. Turn left when you reach the intersection with the Mescal Trail {3} to return to the parking area {1}.

Note: Don't attempt this trail if it is snowy or the trail is icy. There are some places where the trail is narrow with drop offs on the side.

Color Photos: Scan the QR code below for additional color photos of this trail

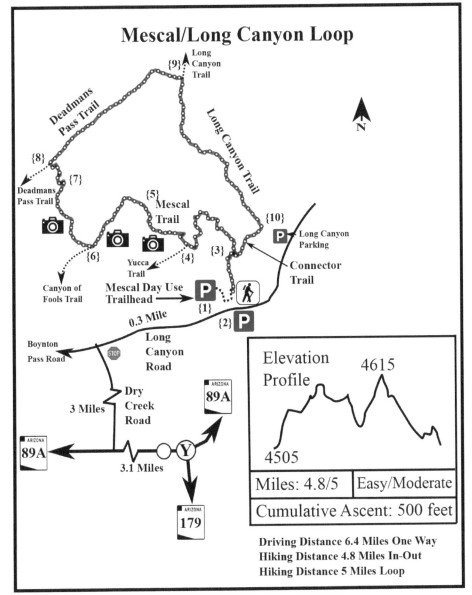

Red Rock State Park Trails

Summary: Red Rock State Park is a 286 acre nature preserve and environmental education center with excellent scenery. It features 10 trails, 7 of which are described below. Hikes led by naturalists are available daily – call the Park at (928) 282-6907

Challenge Level: Easy to Moderate

Hiking Distance:
Varies (see descriptions)

Hiking Time: Varies

Trail Popularity: 🚶🚶🚶

Trailhead Directions: From the "Y" roundabout (see page 7), drive west on SR 89A about 5.5 miles then turn left onto the Lower Red Rock Loop Road. Continue on the Lower Red Rock Loop for 3 miles and turn right at the sign for the Red Rock State Park. You'll come to the entry station. An entry fee is required. (34°49.082'N; 11149.920'W)

Description: Red Rock State Park has 5 miles of maintained trails ranging from easy trails to moderate trails. Descriptions of the most popular trails follows.

Bunkhouse Trail: This easy 0.4 mile loop from the Visitor Center is a good way to get to Kingfisher Bridge, which crosses Oak Creek

Smoke Trail: This easy 0.4 mile trail features a walk along Oak Creek

Yavapai Ridge Trail: This moderate short trail is somewhat hilly. You can access it by crossing Kingfisher Bridge, continuing a short distance on the Apache Fire Trail and then turning left.

Kisva Trail: After crossing Kingfisher Bridge, turn right at the first trail and follow this easy trail along an old ranch road.

Apache Fire Trail: After crossing the Kingfisher Bridge, watch for the Apache Fire loop. This moderate trail includes a possible side trip to the House of Apache Fires.

Javelina Trail: This moderate trail includes scenic overlooks with views of Cathedral Rock.

Eagle's Nest Trail: This moderate trail includes a 200 foot climb. But the views from the vista are very nice and worth the climb.

Color Photos: Scan the QR code below for additional color photos of these trails

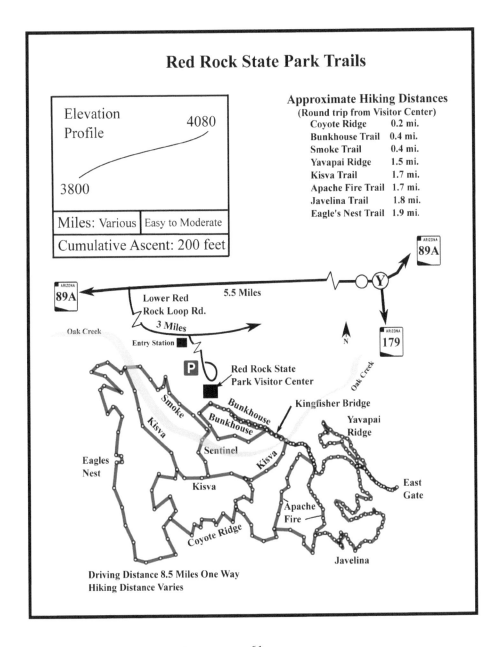

Red Rock State Park Trails

Elevation Profile	4080

3800

Miles: Various	Easy to Moderate

Cumulative Ascent: 200 feet

Approximate Hiking Distances
(Round trip from Visitor Center)

Coyote Ridge	0.2 mi.
Bunkhouse Trail	0.4 mi.
Smoke Trail	0.4 mi.
Yavapai Ridge	1.5 mi.
Kisva Trail	1.7 mi.
Apache Fire Trail	1.7 mi.
Javelina Trail	1.8 mi.
Eagle's Nest Trail	1.9 mi.

ARIZONA 89A

ARIZONA 89A

Lower Red Rock Loop Rd.   5.5 Miles

3 Miles

Oak Creek

Entry Station

N

ARIZONA 179

P

Red Rock State Park Visitor Center

Oak Creek

Smoke

Kisva

Bunkhouse

Bunkhouse

Kingfisher Bridge

Yavapai Ridge

Sentinel

Kisva

Eagles Nest

Kisva

East Gate

Kisva

Apache Fire

Coyote Ridge

Javelina

Driving Distance 8.5 Miles One Way
Hiking Distance Varies

Scheurman Mountain Trail ★

Summary:
A favorite in-out hike up the side of a mountain with great panoramic views of Cathedral Rock and other notable landmarks

Challenge Level:
Moderate

Hiking Distance:
About 0.5 mile to the top then another 0.25 miles to the southern overlook, and another 0.25 mile to the northern overlook or 2 miles round trip

Hiking Time: About 1 ½ hours round trip

Trail Popularity: 🚶🚶

Trailhead Directions: From the "Y" roundabout (see page 7), drive west toward Cottonwood on SR 89A about 4.25 miles. Turn left onto the Upper Red Rock Loop Road. Sedona High School is on your right. Turn right at the third driveway (it's behind the school) then drive past 10 parking places on the left and look for the sign to the trailhead parking area on the left {1}. (34°50.762'N; 111°49.716'W) This parking area also serves the Scorpion and Skywalker Trails.

Description: Scheurman Mountain Trail provides great views of Cathedral Rock and other red rock views to the south. You begin by hiking behind the Red Rock High School where you'll intersect the Scorpion Trail on the left {2} then see a large array of solar panels as big as the school's football field. After 0.2 mile, the trail goes around a gate, placed there when cattle once grazed the area. The trail up is steep in places, so watch your footing. If you hike in April, you may encounter wildflowers blooming.

When you get to the top {3}, you'll see a Scheurman Mountain Trail sign pointing straight ahead (west). I don't recommend hiking this trail because the views are limited. Rather, take the trail to the left (south) marked Scheurman Mt Vista for a good view of Cathedral Rock {4}.

The best views of Cathedral Rock from the southern view point are in the afternoon. You can also take the faint (and unmarked) trail to the right to the top to look northwest toward the Verde Valley and Mingus Mountain {5}. Note that the trail up and on top of Scheurman Mountain is very rocky in places.

Color Photos: Scan the QR code below for additional color photos of this trail

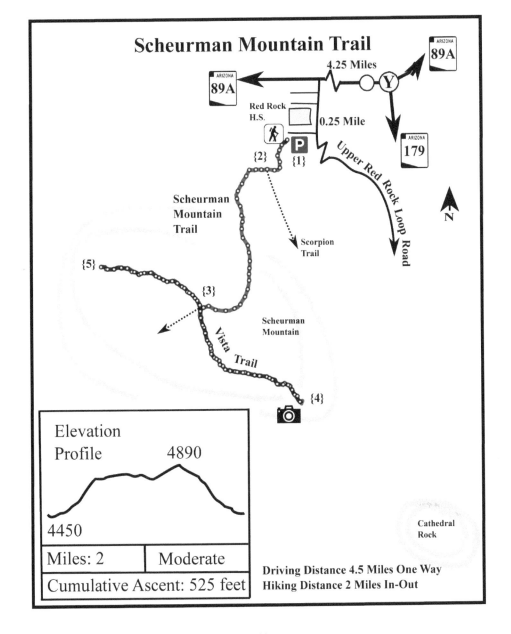

Skywalker/Herkenham Loop

Summary: A loop hike on the western edge of Sedona featuring views of Cathedral Rock, Courthouse Butte and West Sedona

Challenge Level: Moderate

Hiking Distance: About 3.8 mile loop hike

Hiking Time: About 2 ½ hours round trip

Trail Popularity:

Trailhead Directions: From the "Y" roundabout (see page 7), drive west toward Cottonwood on SR 89A about 4.25 miles. Turn left onto the Upper Red Rock Loop Road. Sedona High School is on your right. Turn right at the third driveway (it's behind the school) then drive past 10 parking places on the left and look for the sign to the trailhead parking area on the left {1}. (34°50.762'N; 111°49.716'W) This parking area also serves the Scheurman Mountain and Scorpion Trails. The trail begins across Upper Red Rock Loop Road {2}.

Description: You'll be hiking three trails to complete the loop which are Skywalker, Old Post and Herkenham trails. Skywalker and Herkenham are narrow with ups and downs while Old Post is a gentle downhill hike. An afternoon hike will give you excellent views to the south.

Begin by hiking Skywalker. In 0.2 mile, you'll intersect the Over Easy Trail, which is a little loop trail. You'll intersect it again after 0.5 mile. At 0.7 mile, you'll come to a bench with nice views to the south {3}. Just beyond the bench the trail becomes very narrow with a large drop off for 0.2 mile so watch your footing.

You'll see houses all along the Skywalker Trail but they really don't distract from the pleasant views. At 1.1 miles, you'll come to the highest point on the trail {4} and have a nice view of West Sedona to the north. At 1.3 miles, you'll be under a power line {5}, then in 2 miles you'll intersect the Old Post Trail {6}. Make a right turn here onto the Old Post Trail but look north here for a nice view of Thunder Mountain.

After 0.5 mile, you'll intersect the Carroll Canyon Trail on the left {7}. Continue on the Old Post Trail. You'll intersect the Herkenham Trail at 2.9 miles {8}. Turn right here onto the Herkenham Trail then begin a series of ups and downs as you head northwest. At 3.3 miles, the trail turns left at the bottom of a wash {9}. Continue on Herkenham back to the trailhead {2} and the parking area {1}.

Color Photos: Scan the QR code below for additional color photos of this trail

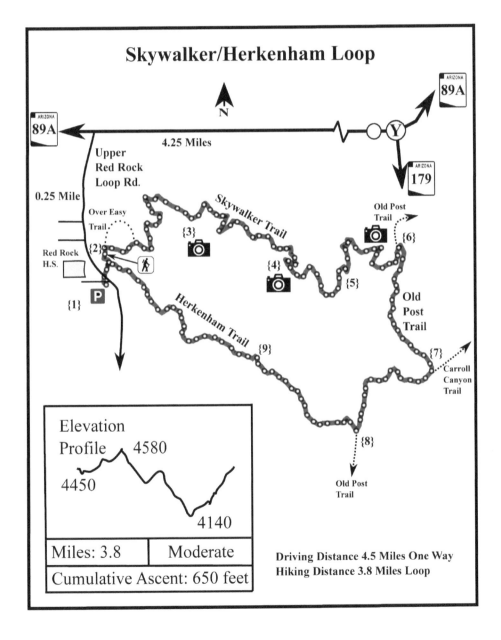

Soldier Pass Trail ★

Summary: A favorite in-out hike with stops at the Devil's Kitchen and the Seven Sacred Pools along with a side trip to some impressive red rock arches

Challenge Level: Moderate

Hiking Distance:
About 2.1 miles one way to the Brins Mesa Trail or 4.2 miles round trip from the trailhead parking lot; add 2.5 miles from the Posse Grounds Park & Ride parking lot

Hiking Time:
About 3 hours round trip or 4 hours from Posse Grounds Park & Ride

Trail Popularity:
👣 👣 👣 👣

Trailhead Directions: From the "Y" roundabout (see page 7), drive west toward Cottonwood on SR 89A for 1.25 miles then turn right onto Soldiers Pass Road. Proceed on Soldiers Pass Road for 1.5 miles. Note Carruth Road on the left after 0.5 mile. Continue another 1 mile and turn right onto Rim Shadows. Go about 0.25 mile then turn left into the parking area {1}. (34°53.057'N; 111°47.028'W)

Parking is very limited at this popular trail. If you are hiking Thursday thru Sunday, you must take the shuttle because the parking area is closed. **(see Trailhead Shuttle Service page 5)** or park at the Posse Grounds Park & Ride lot {9} located on Carruth Road and follow the mixed-use trail along Soldiers Pass Road to reach the Soldier Pass trailhead.

Description: Shortly after beginning the Soldier Pass Trail, you'll descend into the deep Soldier Wash then climb up to the Devil's Kitchen (about 0.2 mile) {2}. This is the largest sinkhole in the Sedona area. After another 0.4 mile, you'll come to the Seven Sacred Pools, which are small depressions in the red rock that hold water even in dry periods {3}. These two areas are very popular with hikers and visitors on jeep rides. You won't encounter jeeps or as many other hikers on the rest of the trail. There is partial shade beginning at about the 1 mile mark and the trees tend to block some of the red rock views.

About 1.3 miles from the trailhead, look to the right for a faint trail up to the Soldier Pass Arches {4}. It's a steep climb of about 275 feet with drop offs so be extremely careful if you attempt to go to the arches {5}. Return to the main trail. As you continue, the trail becomes rockier and steeper as it approaches Brins Mesa. Once on top of Brins Mesa, you'll come to a fork at the 2 mile mark {6}. Take the right fork to an overlook {8} or take the left fork to the intersection with the Brins Mesa Trail after another 0.1 mile {7}. Turn around here, or you can hike a loop by turning right onto the Brins Mesa Trail (see Brins Mesa/Soldier Pass Loop).

Color Photos: Scan the QR code below for additional color photos of this trail

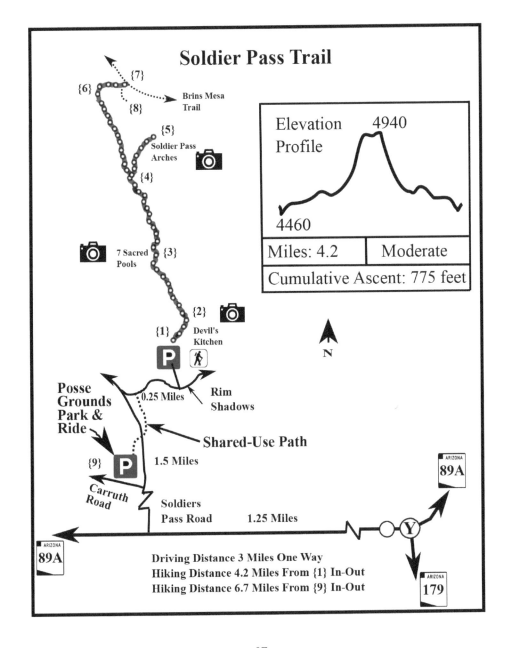

Soldier Pass Trail

{7}

{6}

{8}   Brins Mesa
       Trail

{5}
Soldier Pass
Arches

{4}

Elevation   4940
Profile

4460

Miles: 4.2	Moderate
Cumulative Ascent: 775 feet	

7 Sacred   {3}
Pools

{2}

{1}   Devil's
       Kitchen

P **🚶**

N

Posse
Grounds
Park &
Ride

0.25 Miles   Rim
              Shadows

Shared-Use Path

{9} **P**   1.5 Miles

Carruth
Road   Soldiers
            Pass Road   1.25 Miles

ARIZONA
89A

ARIZONA
89A

Y

Driving Distance 3 Miles One Way
Hiking Distance 4.2 Miles From {1} In-Out
Hiking Distance 6.7 Miles From {9} In-Out

ARIZONA
179

Soldier Wash Trails
Grand Central/Javelina Loop

Summary: A loop hike that passes a beautiful overlook with wonderful views

Challenge Level: Moderate

Hiking Distance: About a 5 mile loop

Hiking Time: About 2 ½ hours round trip

Trail Popularity: 🚶🚶

Trailhead Directions: From the "Y" roundabout (see page 7), drive towards Cottonwood 0.8 mile then turn right into the small parking area along SR 89A. {1} (34°51.908'N; 111°46.593'W) There are only 5 parking spaces here but you can squeeze in 2 more vehicles

Description: There are seven connecting trails within the Soldier Wash Trail System. This is a loop by hiking up the center of the system on the Grand Central Trail, stopping at a beautiful overlook then continuing back on the east side via the Javelina Trail. The views improve the further north you hike.

From the parking area, follow the signs for the Adobe Jack Trail. After 350 feet, you descend into a large wash then hike up to make a sharp right turn onto the Crusty Trail. As you proceed, you cross back and forth and hike in the wash for a large part of the way. After 0.6 mile, you'll intersect the Grand Central Trail (GCT) {2}. Make a left turn then begin hiking north for 1.4 miles. The GCT is very shaded for the first 0.5 mile. As you hike along, you'll intersect the Coyote, Power Line Plunge and Shorty Trails. When you intersect the Ant Hill Loop Trail, turn left; walk 7 paces then turn right to continue on the GCT. The trail now becomes steep and there is loose rock so watch your footing. After 0.1 mile, look to the left for a high red rock knoll known as Ant Hill which is a great place to stop for photos and a snack {3}. You'll have 360 degree views and can see Bell Rock, Courthouse Butte, Sugarloaf, Chimney Rock, Snoopy, Lucy and other Sedona landmarks. If you like, this is a good place to turn around and return to the parking area for a 4 mile round trip hike.

To hike the loop, continue north on the GCT for 0.3 mile then make a right turn onto the Ant Hill Loop Trail {4}. Follow the Ant Hill Loop Trail for 0.2 mile then make a right turn (east) onto the Jordan Trail {5}. Follow the Jordan Trail for 0.5 mile then turn right (south) onto the Javelina Trail {6}. Follow the Javelina Trail for 1.2 miles then turn right (west) onto the GCT {7}. Follow the GCT for 0.1 mile then continue on the Crusty Trail {2} for 0.6 mile back to the parking area {1}.

Color Photos: Scan the QR code below for additional color photos of this trail

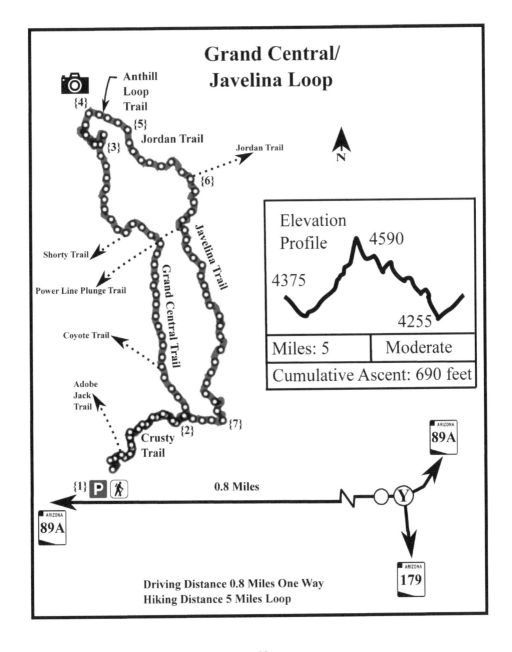

Grand Central/ Javelina Loop

Anthill Loop Trail {4} {5}

Jordan Trail {3}

Jordan Trail {6}

Shorty Trail

Power Line Plunge Trail

Javelina Trail

Grand Central Trail

Coyote Trail

Adobe Jack Trail

Crusty Trail {2} {7}

{1} P

Elevation Profile 4590
4375
4255

| Miles: 5 | Moderate |

Cumulative Ascent: 690 feet

ARIZONA 89A

ARIZONA 89A

0.8 Miles

Y

ARIZONA 179

Driving Distance 0.8 Miles One Way
Hiking Distance 5 Miles Loop

Templeton Trail

Summary: An in-out hike with views of Sedona's major rock formations

Challenge Level: Moderate

Hiking Distance: About 4.1 miles each way from the Court House Vista parking area to the intersection of the Baldwin Loop Trail; about 8.2 miles round trip

Hiking Time: About 5 hours as an in-out hike from the Court House Vista parking area to the intersection of the Baldwin Loop Trail and return

Trail Popularity: 🏃🏃 🏃🏃 🏃🏃

Trailhead Directions: From the "Y" roundabout (see page 7), drive south on SR 179 for about 5 miles to the parking area. After you drive about 3.2 miles, just past the Back O' Beyond roundabout, SR 179 becomes a divided highway. Continue driving south. About 1.8 miles beyond the Back O' Beyond roundabout, southbound SR 179 adds a passing lane on the left. From the passing lane, turn left at the sign for the Court House Vista parking area {1}. (34°48.350'N; 111°46.009'W) Before you turn, you'll see Bell Rock ahead of you on the left side of SR 179. There are toilets at the parking area. This parking area also serves the Bell Rock, Llama and Courthouse Butte Loop Trails. The trail starts just beyond the interpretive signboard.

Description: The Templeton Trail extends northwest from the Bell Rock Pathway, just north of Bell Rock and Courthouse Butte to the Baldwin Loop trail near Oak Creek and Red Rock Crossing. It provides excellent views of Bell Rock, Courthouse Butte, Lee Mountain, Cathedral Rock and many other rock formations. You can access the east end of the Templeton Trail {6} from the Baldwin Loop parking area {7}.

If you hike from the Court House Vista parking area, which most people do, look for the Phone Trail on your left about 25 feet past the interpretive signboard {2}. Follow the Phone Trail 0.3 mile then continue north (left) on the Bell Rock Pathway Trail. In 0.1 mile turn left onto the Templeton Trail {3} then follow it beneath both the northbound and southbound lanes of SR 179. You'll have excellent views of Cathedral Rock ahead and, in 1 mile, you'll intersect the HT Trail on your right {4}. As you approach Cathedral Rock, the landscape becomes high desert.

You'll intersect the Cathedral Rock Trail in another 1.3 miles on your right {5} and the short but steep trail to the saddle of Cathedral Rock in another 200 feet on your left. As you continue on the Templeton Trail, you'll descend a series of switchbacks. In 0.8 mile, you'll be adjacent to Oak Creek, across from Buddha Beach and Red Rock Crossing. The Templeton Trail continues on for another 0.2 mile where it ends at the Baldwin Loop trail {6}. Turn around here for a hike of 8.2 miles. The Baldwin Loop Trail parking area is another 0.5 mile further {7}.

Color Photos: Scan the QR code below for additional color photos of this trail

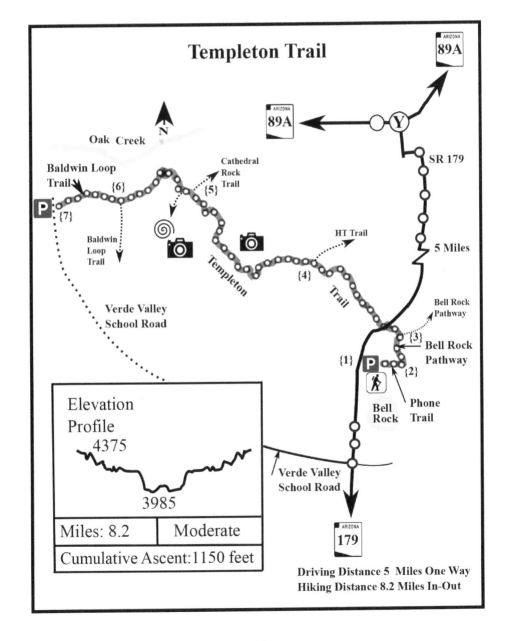

Thunder Mountain/Andante Loop ★

Summary:
A favorite sunny in-town hike with excellent views

Challenge Level:
Moderate

Hiking Distance:
About 3 miles loop

Hiking Time:
About 2 hours round trip

Trail Popularity:

Trailhead Directions: From the "Y" roundabout (see page 7), drive west toward Cottonwood on SR 89A about 3 miles. Turn right onto Dry Creek Road then proceed for 0.5 mile. Turn right onto Thunder Mountain Road then drive 0.7 mile. The parking area is on your left {1}. (34°52.325'N; 111°48.735'W) This parking area also serves the Chimney Rock Upper and Lower Loop. The entrance gate opens each day at 8:00 am; the exit gate is never closed. You can also park at the Coffeepot, Sugarloaf, Teacup Trail parking area

Description: From the parking area, go west past the signboard for about 100 feet then turn right onto the Lower Chimney Trail. In 0.1 miles, you'll come to the intersection of the Thunder Mountain Trail {2}. Turn right onto the Thunder Mountain Trail and you'll soon intersect a social trail after 0.4 mile {3}. After another 0.1 mile, you'll intersect the Andante Trail {4}. Turn right here and follow the Andante Trail. You'll be following overhead power lines and see many rooftops to the south. But the views are excellent to the north. After 0.6 mile, you'll come to the Andante Road parking area {5} and be next to a large green water tank. Continue across the access road and at 0.8 mile you'll come to a nice scenic area {6}. At 1.25 miles, you'll intersect the Thunder Mountain Trail which is the end of the Andante Trail. {7}.

If you follow the Thunder Mountain Trail to the right (east), you'll intersect the Teacup Trail in 0.25 mile. Rather than that, continue straight ahead and follow the Thunder Mountain Trail west. The views along this portion of Thunder Mountain Trail are excellent and there are no rooftops in view. There are some narrow portions of the trail here so watch your footing. At 2 miles, you'll come to a huge rock along the trail {8}.

You'll come to the intersection of the Thunder Mountain and Chimney Pass Trails after 2.5 miles {9}. Make a left here and continue south on the Thunder Mountain Trail back to the parking area to complete the 3 mile loop.

Note: This trail has little shade so it will be a hot hike in the summer.

Color Photos: Scan the QR code below for additional color photos of this trail

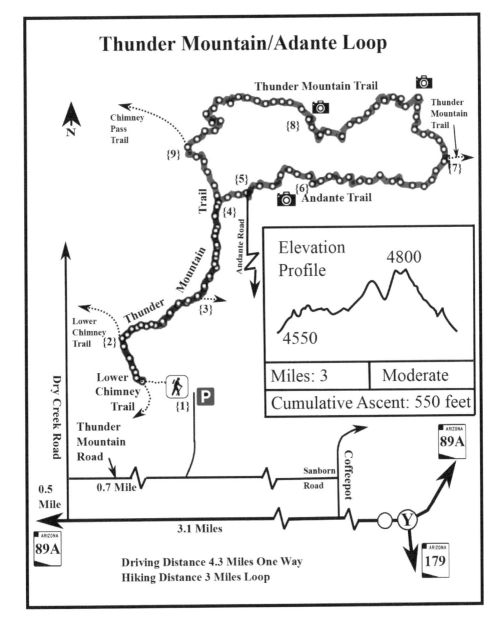

Thunder Mountain/Adante Loop

N

Thunder Mountain Trail

Chimney
Pass
Trail

Thunder
Mountain
Trail

{9}

{8}

{7}

{5}

{6}

Andante Trail

{4}

Thunder Mountain Trail

Andante Road

{3}

Lower
Chimney
Trail {2}

Lower
Chimney
Trail {1}

Elevation Profile

4800

4550

Miles: 3	Moderate
Cumulative Ascent: 550 feet	

Thunder
Mountain
Road

Dry Creek Road

Sanborn
Road

Coffeepot

ARIZONA
89A

0.5
Mile

0.7 Mile

3.1 Miles

Y

ARIZONA
89A

ARIZONA
179

Driving Distance 4.3 Miles One Way
Hiking Distance 3 Miles Loop

West Fork Trail ★

Summary:
A favorite, shady in-out hike along the West Fork of Oak Creek

Challenge Level:
Moderate

Hiking Distance:
About 3.6 miles each way or 7.2 miles round trip

Hiking Time:
About 4 hours round trip

Trail Popularity: 🚶🚶 🚶🚶 🚶🚶 🚶🚶

Trailhead Directions: From the "Y" roundabout (see page 7), drive north on SR 89A about 10.5 miles. Turn left into the parking area {1}. (34°59.446'N; 111°44.570'W) If left turns are prohibited into the parking area, continue north on SR 89A for 1.2 miles and turn around at the Cave Springs campground. The trail starts on the far side of the parking area, furthest away from the entrance. There are toilets at the parking area. The gate to the parking area opens at 8:00 am. It is a special fee area (see Red Rock Pass Fee Program, page 11). The parking area fills quickly so arrive early in the morning.

Description: West Fork is considered by many to be the most beautiful trail in the Sedona area. You'll be crossing the water 13 times as you hike the trail. You have to step from stone to stone to cross, so the trail isn't recommended in high water times (you'll get your feet wet!).

After 0.3 mile, you'll come to the remains of Mayhew's Lodge, built in the 1880s. It was remodeled in 1895 then burned down in 1980 {2}. At the 0.4 mile mark, you'll come to the first of the 13 creek crossings {3}.

As you continue along, look to the sides for some amazing red rock bluffs. There is a nice spot to stop and enjoy the creek after 1.1 miles {4}. At 2.8 miles, the trail is next to a large overhang where the water has eroded the rock {5}. Walk about 25 feet west toward the creek and look down. This is a nice place for a break. Continue another 0.4 mile and watch for a short side trail to a cave on your left {6}. At 3.6 miles, you'll come to a sign marking the end of the trail {7}. Sometimes you can continue a little further, depending on the water level but usually you'll have to wade through the water to go further.

West Fork has two wonderful seasons, spring and fall. The most beautiful is fall, when the deciduous trees display glorious colors. The third or fourth week in October seems to be when the colors are usually at their peak.

Color Photos: Scan the QR code below for additional color photos of this trail

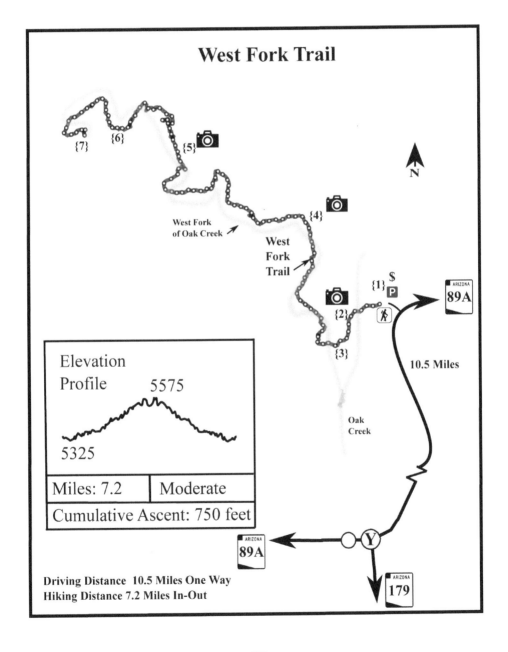

West Fork Trail

West Fork
of Oak Creek

West
Fork
Trail

{1}

{2}

{3}

{4}

{5}

{6}

{7}

N

ARIZONA
89A

10.5 Miles

Oak
Creek

Elevation
Profile   5575

5325

Miles: 7.2	Moderate
Cumulative Ascent: 750 feet	

ARIZONA
89A

Y

ARIZONA
179

Driving Distance 10.5 Miles One Way
Hiking Distance 7.2 Miles In-Out

Wilson Canyon Trail ★

Summary:
A favorite in-out hike in a shaded canyon with limited red rock views

Challenge Level:
Moderate

Hiking Distance:
About 1.3 miles each way or 2.6 miles round trip

Hiking Time:
About 2 hours round trip

Trail Popularity: 🚶🚶🚶

Trailhead Directions: From the "Y" roundabout (see page 7), drive north on SR 89A to Midgley Bridge. The trailhead parking is on your left just after you cross the bridge {1}. (34°54.023'N; 111°44.901'W) There are only 13 parking spots plus 1 handicapped spot so the parking area can fill up quickly on the weekends. There is a toilet near the parking area.

Description: The trail begins away from SR 89A at the far end of the parking area, just beyond the picnic table pavilion. In about 100 feet, just past the toilet, you'll come to a metal sign for the Wilson Mountain (South) Trail on the right {2}. Continue straight ahead for about 0.1 mile then bear right at the fork in the trail and the signpost {3}. At first, the trail is wide but narrows further on. At about 0.5 mile, you'll come to a second, wooden sign for the Wilson Mountain Trail on the right {4}. You'll intersect the end of the Jim Thompson Trail in another 300 feet {5}.

The Wilson Canyon Trail crosses the wash at the bottom of the canyon 13 times as it winds back and forth for 1.3 miles. You'll be hiking among scrub oak and small Arizona cypress. The trail becomes somewhat narrow with large drop offs about 1 mile in.

After 1.3 miles, you'll come to a 3 foot tall cairn (and is the only cairn you'll find after passing the Jim Thompson Trail {5}) that sometimes has a sign End of Trail on it marking the end of the official trail. Stop here or continue up the wash for another 75 feet. Watch for a steep side trail on your right {6}. Scramble up onto the nearby rock outcropping for some terrific views all around {7}. About 20 paces beyond the cairn, you'll see what looks like a continuation of the trail. But it only goes 50 feet or so then drops back into the wash.

Color Photos: Scan the QR code below for additional color photos of this trail

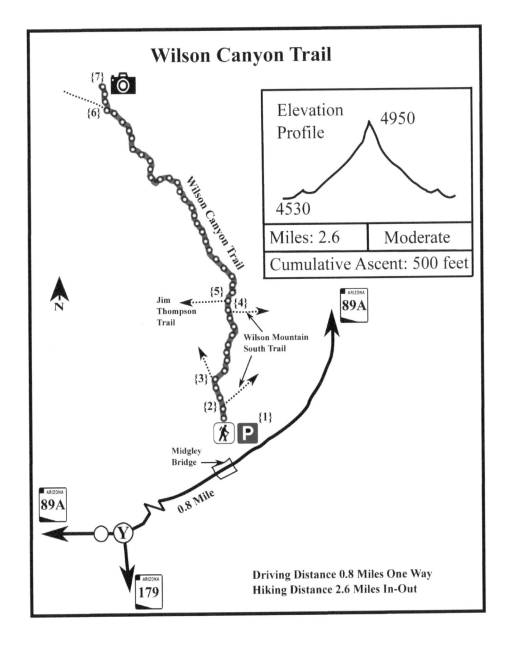

Wilson Canyon Trail

{7}

{6}

Wilson Canyon Trail

Elevation Profile

4950

4530

Miles: 2.6	Moderate
Cumulative Ascent: 500 feet	

{5}

Jim
Thompson
Trail

{4}

N

ARIZONA
89A

Wilson Mountain
South Trail

{3}

{2}

{1}

P

Midgley
Bridge

ARIZONA
89A

0.8 Mile

Y

ARIZONA
179

Driving Distance 0.8 Miles One Way
Hiking Distance 2.6 Miles In-Out

Beyond the Hike

Here's a list of things to see and do around Sedona when you aren't out on the trail.

Airport Overlook - Atop Airport Mesa is a scenic overlook, which provides magnificent views of Coffeepot Rock, Thunder Mountain, Sugarloaf and Chimney Rock. Looking west across the Verde Valley, you'll see the Black Hills; on a clear day you can even see the "J" above Jerome, Arizona to the west.

From the "Y" roundabout, drive west toward Cottonwood on SR 89A for 1 mile then turn left onto Airport Road. Proceed up Airport Road for 1.1 miles to the parking area on your left. Once you have parked, cross the road and enjoy the view. There is a $3 parking fee here.

Chapel of the Holy Cross - The Chapel of the Holy Cross is a local landmark and a must see. It was opened in 1956 and serves as a place to meditate and enjoy the beauty that is Sedona. There is no charge to park or enter but they gladly accept donations.

From the "Y" roundabout, proceed south on SR 179 to the Chapel Road roundabout. Take the third exit and proceed east on Chapel Road to the end. The driveway and sidewalk up to the Chapel are somewhat steep. The Chapel has a gift shop located in the lower level.

Oak Creek Canyon - The drive up Oak Creek Canyon is a world-famous route. It can be very busy on weekends and holidays. You begin in Sedona and drive toward Flagstaff to the Scenic View Area, just past the Switchbacks. This beautiful canyon, created over millions of years, features beautiful views. Cell phone reception can be limited in Oak Creek Canyon. You'll climb in elevation from about 4500 feet (Sedona) to about 6400 feet (at the Scenic View Area).

From the "Y" roundabout, proceed north on SR 89A through Uptown Sedona. If taking photographs, be sure you pull off the road far enough to let vehicles pass by. Drive up Oak Creek Canyon for 16 miles then turn right into the Scenic View Area.

Crescent Moon Ranch/Red Rock Crossing - Crescent Moon Ranch/Red Rock Crossing is where you can stroll along the banks of Oak Creek and take amazing photographs of Cathedral Rock with the creek in the foreground, one of the most recognized photographic settings in Sedona. Be sure to go in the afternoon for the best photographs. This is a special fee area (see page 9).

From the "Y" roundabout, drive west on SR 89A about 4.25 miles then turn left onto the Upper Red Rock Loop Road. Follow the Upper Red Rock Loop Road for about 1.9 miles for the best views. If you want to continue to Crescent Moon Ranch/Red Rock Crossing, turn left onto Chavez Ranch Road then follow it about 1 mile to the end until you reach the entrance gate.

V-Bar-V Heritage Site - There are more than 1000 images created by the Native peoples from about AD 1100 to 1300 at V-Bar-V. It is an easy 0.5 mile hike from the Visitor Center to the rock art. Note: The site is normally open Friday through Monday, 9:30 am to 3:00 pm, but you should check with the Sedona Chamber of Commerce Visitor Center, the Red Rock Ranger Station or call (928) 592-0998 for days of operation. A Red Rock Pass or equivalent is required to park. Pets are not allowed on the site.

From the "Y" roundabout, drive south on SR 179 about 14.75 miles to the intersection of Interstate 17. Drive under I-17 then continue for another 2.75 miles on the paved Forest Road 618. Turn right into the parking area.

Sedona Heritage Museum – The Sedona Heritage Museum is housed in the former orchard and home of Walter and Ruth Jordan. Here you can learn about the pioneers of the Sedona area, from the 1870s through the heyday of western film-making in the 1950s.

From the "Y" roundabout, drive north on SR 89A about 0.3 mile to the Jordan Road roundabout. Take the third exit onto Jordan Road then drive ¾ mile to the parking area on the left. Call (928) 282-7038 for information on special programs. Leashed pets permitted.

Other Titles by the Author

Hiking the Vortexes, B & W Edition   *Hiking the Vortexes, Color Edition*

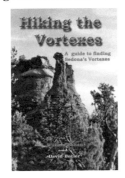

Sedona Relocation Guide

Index

The Author and Niece Standing on Devil's Bridge